Breaking Free of Bonkers

Breaking Free of Bonkers

How to Lead in Today's Crazy World of Organizations

George Binney, Philip Glanfield,
Gerhard Wilke

NICHOLAS BREALEY
PUBLISHING

London • Boston

First published in Great Britain in 2017 by Nicholas Brealey Publishing
An imprint of John Murray Press
An Hachette UK Company

1

© George Binney, Philip Glanfield, Gerhard Wilke 2017

The right of George Binney, Philip Glanfield and Gerhard Wilke to
be identified as the Authors of the Work has been asserted by them in
accordance with the Copyright, Designs and Patents Act 1988.

A CIP catalogue record for this title is available from the British Library

Hardback ISBN 978-1-47366-907-9
Ebook ISBN (UK) 978-1-47367-059-4
Ebook ISBN (US) 978-1-47366-995-6

Typeset in Bembo MT by Hewer Text UK Ltd, Edinburgh
Printed and bound by Clays Ltd, St Ives plc

Nicholas Brealey policy is to use papers that are natural, renewable and
recyclable products and made from wood grown in sustainable forests.
The logging and manufacturing processes are expected to conform
to the environmental regulations of the country of origin.

Nicholas Brealey Publishing
John Murray Press
Carmelite House
50 Victoria Embankment
London EC4Y 0DZ, UK
Tel: 020 3122 6000

Nicholas Brealey Publishing
Hachette Book Group
Market Place Center, 53 State Street
Boston, MA 02109, USA
Tel: (617) 263 1834

www.nicholasbrealey.com

Contents

PART 3 – Breaking Free of Bonkers

INTRODUCTION

Why This Book, and Why Now?

'Bonkers' is a provocative word. In our day-to-day conversation we use it with a shrug of the shoulders. We dismiss some aspect of the world as crazy or perverse and we are, at the same time, accepting that we can't change it. Bonkers is the way of the world . . .

The title of this book was prompted by a chief executive who, in a candid moment, told us that his job was to work with the 'bonkers' – to make sense of an insane world; to do a good job against the odds.

In our job as organization consultants, we have met many people, in many different fields, who are bewildered and oppressed by the apparent insanity of much of what goes on in organizations. There are seemingly endless reorganizations and restructurings. Leaders feel they need to disturb people and organizations. People are sometimes not sure what unit they are part of, or who their boss is. They seem to serve computer systems rather than the other way round, and spend inordinate amounts of time ticking boxes and preparing plans and policies that don't make a difference, as well as sitting in unproductive meetings. The time to do real work is squeezed, organizations are hollowed out; there are lots of controls but little trust. Culture is seen as a problem – a barrier to much needed change – and we are asked to put our faith in abstract ideas that bear little relationship to reality. There is so much that is bonkers. Maybe we need to take it more seriously.

The origins of bonkers

Our view is that a *heroic* orthodoxy – embracing ideas of leadership, change and strategy – has come to dominate organizational life since the Thatcher/Reagan revolution in the late 1970s and the 1980s. The orthodoxy is that, in a period of unprecedented upheaval, the job of leaders is to drive through change. The orthodoxy assumes that 'business knows best', and was promoted by many business schools and consultancies, used first in the private sector, and then extended to the public sector. The approach is credited with many of the remarkable achievements of modern organizations.

However, every way of seeing is also a way of *not* seeing. Every way of doing is a way of *not* doing. Many of the costs and frustrations of organizational life today stem from being tied to just one way of thinking about (and working with) organizations and people. The top-down managerial efforts at change that come with the orthodoxy, however well intentioned, keep producing unintended consequences.

The orthodoxy derives from a long-standing neo-liberal picture of society (a picture which is now being challenged by 'Brexit' and Donald Trump as well as the Left). The neo-liberal view is that the best way to make sense of what humans do is an economist's model. We are economic animals, who will respond to 'rational' incentives, carrots and sticks. This is one, narrow version of liberalism, perverted into a kind of fundamentalism; a claim that there is only one truth in society – the free market, choice and competition. Leaders, it is believed, must wrestle organizations into shape to fit this idealized model.

The heroic approach is all around us. It is so much the orthodoxy that many managers and leaders take it for granted. It is the sea we swim in and cannot see.

Faced by this orthodoxy and the bonkers it creates, we each have a choice about how to respond.

Do we keep our heads down and go into survival mode? Do we revolt? Or can we recover the capacity in our working lives to think, feel and act for ourselves? That's the path we suggest in this book.

We offer our direct experience of people who work productively and lead well, *despite* the orthodoxy. They have broken free of bonkers. They know (often intuitively) from their experience what makes sense. We tell their stories and offer their insights, describing how:

- They recognize that good management is essential but effective leadership comes first.

- They trust their own experience, feelings and intuition as much as their intellect.

- They focus on connecting with the people around them and not just on the task.

- They reach out to others and focus on 'we' not 'I', recognizing that liberating the collective intelligence of groups and organizations is more important than any one person's contribution.

- They work with the grain of what they have. They are respectful of what exists and what has gone before, and do not throw it all up in the air.

- They see the potential in every situation and interaction to make a difference; they don't postpone effective action to some glittering future that never arrives.

The alternatives to the heroic orthodoxy are not new. One of the aspects of current business and management culture that most disturbs us is the absence of a sense of history. We want to recover old wisdom, which we are all aware of at some level, going back to the Enlightenment and the Scientific Revolution and before.

It seems to us essential to restore some old insights. We are much more than rational, economic animals. We are social beings shaped by history and culture – indeed, being 'rational' is only rational if it takes this context into consideration, otherwise it's bonkers!

Organizations are communities (not economists' models or machines) which have grown up over a period of time and as a result of many influences; they are not the result of any overall design. They deserve respect. We need to start with curiosity about the specific history and context of each organization, and pay close attention to purpose, meaning and social attachment.

We argue that we should apply to business and organizations the same principles of pluralism that should apply (in liberal democratic countries) in society as a whole – that there is no one answer to all problems and we should consider issues from a range of perspectives; that there should be checks and balances (and that no one person or group should have too much power); and that open debate and the free exchange of ideas and information are essential to progress.

We are under no illusions. With such a dominant and complete orthodoxy that purports to explain all organizational life, it is difficult to make space for an alternative view.

What we want to do in this book is to encourage you to break free of the bonkers by finding the gaps, cracks and opportunities that exist in any supposedly complete belief system. We want to offer hope and encouragement to those who go about leading in a different way.

There are different ways of working and leading. We know from our work the potential for people in organizations to be very different; to recover their wits and be potent. We encourage you to take your experience seriously; to restore judgement and value intuition. We have seen again and again how individuals, groups and organizations can come alive when they free themselves from the heroic orthodoxy and are more able to be themselves, as part of some wider entity. The benefits in terms of happier, more effective people, and more successful organizations, are huge.

4

Who are we?

We have an unusual vantage point. We are organization consultants who together have over 100 years' experience of organizational life as managers, leaders and consultants, in private and
public sectors, in the UK, Germany, Scandinavia and around the
world. We work with individuals and teams at all levels, in many
different companies and organizations. We come alongside chief
executives and boards, middle managers and those in the front
line. We work with senior managers as executive coaches and hear
the 'up close and personal' version of what is happening. We
know what it feels like to lead and manage. We speak not from
theory but from careful attention to experience – to what works
in practice. That experience makes us determined to speak about
what we have found, so you too can lead in a bonkers world.

Your guide to the book

Since the 1980s an 'unholy trinity' of ideas about leadership,
change and strategy has shaped how we think and act in organizations. Leadership, it is assumed, is for a few charismatic, magical
individuals who are capable of implementing change by inspiring
others. Strategy, too, is the job of a few clever, highly paid senior
leaders at the top of the organization. The impressive range of
technology and data that we have at our disposal enables us to run
processes and logistics consistently around the world. It encourages us to believe that we live in an age of rational management in
which all that matters is our ability to reason our way forward,
and that organizations and cultures can be transformed by design.

In this book we offer a different perspective that depends on
recovering our sense of history, humanity and connectedness.

Full of real-life experience and insight, the book is divided into
three parts, which should be read sequentially for maximum
value.

Part 1 (beginning) – Is Everything Bonkers?

In Chapter 1 we suggest that we are probably not alone in finding aspects of today's organizations 'bonkers' – and why that might be so. In Chapter 2 we argue that, by stealth, management has replaced leadership. We need to recover the idea that leadership is an ordinary, social process that is a necessary precondition for effective management. In Chapter 3 we suggest that we have become addicted to the idea of transformational change – an idea which ignores history and is heavily dependent on an idealized future – and individual heroic leaders. We need to recover our sense of connection to each other, our shared history and our experience of the present moment. In Chapter 4 we argue that the holy grail of strategy is just that, an idealized fantasy about the world as it should be; a fantasy which is quickly undone in the messiness of the world as it is.

Part 2 (middle) – Becoming the Leader You Can Be

If our view of leadership, change and strategy makes sense, how can we do well? We suggest that first we need to pay attention to who we are and what we aspire to be part of creating (Chapter 5). To be part of something requires us to develop a sense of meaning and purpose with others in the many groups of which we are part (Chapter 6). More than that, the groups of which we are part need to hold their integrity while connecting their work to other groups as part of a purposeful community (Chapter 7).

In Chapters 8 and 9 we seek to recover some important aspects of organizational life that are denigrated by the current ortho- doxy. It is hopelessly idealistic to 'keep politics out of it', as we often hear. We argue that politics is not a dirty word and that effective leaders appreciate and work the politics of their organi- zation with integrity. By working with politics we establish the connections and relationships that in turn create the environment in which progressive change can occur. Moving from the macro politics of an organization, in Chapter 9 we turn our attention to the micro – the much maligned, seemingly endless meetings that are so characteristic of modern organizational life. How can we recover the meeting as purposeful work?

Part 3 (end) – Breaking Free of Bonkers

In Chapters 10–12 we draw the book together. Chapter 10 illustrates how to break free of bonkers with a single story of leadership, change and strategy. In Chapter 11 we focus on how we can make a difference, and in Chapter 12 we suggest that we need to recover our humanity in the world of organizations.

Our method is consistent with our message. Throughout the book we tell stories drawn from our own and others' experience, as well as provide practical exercises to help you reflect on your own story, or experience. We want to encourage you to pay attention to the stories that you and others tell about yourself and the situation you are in. These stories *are* your leadership. They *are* the culture of your organization and as such both create and limit your potential. Stories recover our sense of history, purpose, context and, most importantly, humanity. Stories are an important counter-weight to the metrics, plans and other abstract representations of organizational life. Stories keep us connected to the world as it is and the help we can get from our colleagues. Stories can help us thrive in a bonkers world.

PART 1

Is Everything Bonkers?

CHAPTER 1

Is It Just Me?

Spend any amount of time working in any organization and it is likely that you will be asking yourself this question: 'Is it just me, or is everything bonkers?' Something will strike you as odd, ridiculous, or just plain bonkers. Is it just me?

Spend any amount of time on the phone to a call centre trying to resolve what seems to you a trivial matter and find yourself on hold, transferred . . . or is it just me? And yet . . . we know it when we see it.

We know it when we see it

Sometimes in our day-to-day lives, perhaps at a time when we need it most, we encounter a group of people who achieve remarkable things in their work. I did not know that Mother and Baby Units existed until someone close to me needed one. Here is a place where the work is unimaginably delicate. Anxious, distressed, depressed, even psychotic, mothers with their newborn babies, who may harm themselves or their babies, and are in need of close personal supervision and care at the same time.

The place itself is secure, and yet even the first encounter on the intercom is welcoming. They know who you are straight away, whether you are expected or whether they need to check with the mother that a visit is welcome. There are protocols and rules, for example, about the level of supervision each mother receives. These are explicit, not hidden, and discussed with the mother on a regular basis. It seems that each member of staff knows what they need to know so questions are not repeated. Their shared dedication is to support the relationship between mother and baby, and to build up the mother's confidence. The boundaries are clear and within those boundaries choices are offered so the mother is always in charge as far as possible. Nothing is too much trouble. When you are leaving for an overnight stay there is a caring check, 'Have you got; do you need?', and an utterly supportive 'If you need us at any time, day or night, just call.'

All of this is visible and could be, perhaps is, written down somewhere – but that is not the point. What mothers, babies and those close to them experience is a place of absolute safety and security when it seems that everything is falling apart. It is a sanctuary. The physical building matters, but you have the sense that the 'sanctuary' lives in this group of staff – they create and hold it between them. You can touch and feel it. Just as a visitor, any new staff member must sense that there is something substantial and precious here, not to be tampered with lightly. To an outsider this strength is remarkable; I imagine to an insider 'it's just the way we do things around here'.

This is an intimate story concerning a life-changing experience. In much more commonplace ways, modern organizations are remarkable, collective achievements that we tend to take for granted. Supermarkets offer us goods from around the world, when we want them, and at high quality and low cost. Google lets us find (with the touch of a finger) information which years ago was buried in some archive. The book or gadget that we want, sometimes need, is delivered the next day. If we are unfortunate enough to be in an accident, emergency services arrive quickly. Hospitals improve and save lives every day, conquering conditions and diseases that a short time ago were disabling or killers.

We only have to step back for a moment to realize that what seems ordinary now is actually the product of remarkable collective human endeavour. The organizations that enable these services have grown up over years. They function in complex and subtle ways. They have a life and cultures that go well beyond the formal organization charts or strategy plans. Most remarkable of all, they work (on the whole!) and have made our lives safer and more comfortable.

And yet, 'Is it just me?' doesn't go away. It seems that all of this comes at a price, and there's much that goes on now in organizational life that is maddening and oppressive.

Permanent restructuring and upheaval

Just as night follows day, a dip in performance, a crisis, a change at the top, a new strategy or product, a retirement or promotion seems to make a restructuring inevitable, and one succeeds another. Before people have got used to the previous reorganization – and long before anyone can judge if the reorganization makes sense – the next one arrives. They pile up like layers of sediment in the river. It's bonkers!

Organizations need to adapt and change as their environments shift. From time to time reorganizations are needed. Yet, now we live in a time of constant structural change. In a previous book written by two of the authors, *Living Leadership*, we call it 'Permanent Transition'. Though transitions are a normal part of human life and essential to the renewal of organizations, the speed and frequency of organizational transitions seems unnatural and counter-productive. It's as if we had to move house, change jobs or face the death of a close relative every month. Just when relationships are developing and the social fabric on which organizations depend for their success is growing, everyone has to start again. The costs to individuals and to organizations are high.

I was talking to an administrator about work we needed to do together. I said that I thought she had done a brilliant job on a previous project. Suddenly she started crying: 'No one here has said that to me recently. All we get from our managers is pressure to do more work. No one appreciates us.'

Tick-box madness

Checklists are useful when flying planes and in an operating theatre. However, the drive to prevent the recurrence of scandals ('LIBOR' dishonesty in banking, 'mis-selling' in pensions, car emissions frauds and appalling care at 'Mid Staffs' hospital) has led to more and more inquiries, regulation and management systems. 'I've done it, take my word for it' is an endangered sentence in organizational life. It's not enough to do the task, you must *prove* that you have done it, and done it correctly. As a result more and more people spend more and more time preparing plans and reports, and have less and less time to do their work. There is a tsunami of policies and procedures that seek to regulate how work is done – more and more 'oughts', with less and less impact on how the work actually gets done. Teachers, policemen, psychiatrists, financial advisers, nurses, doctors, researchers – all are caught up in the paperchase and 'Feeding the Beast'.

The tick box has become the symbol of the age – people going through the motions of applying whatever new policy or initiative is in vogue but losing sight of what it is for. Diversity, fairness, quality, service, safety, accountability, transparency – a million new initiatives have been launched in their name. Nice idea, yes. But what is the reality of implementation? The half-day training is provided. Staff and managers troop through the sheep dip – but does anything really change?

Tick-box madness

Lars, the Swedish CEO of a consumer products multinational company, impressed us enormously. Despite sitting at the top of a huge international organization (with over 50,000 employees), he was remarkably human and unpretentious. He had worked his way up through the company and was very effective in communicating with managers at all levels around the world. He had a clear vision and seemed well equipped to make it happen.

He saw that the company needed to be much more innovative. The company had a great brand, but most of its products were mature and competition was challenging – both from the Far East in low-cost segments and from Europe in high-value/stylish segments. But how do you make a huge international company more innovative?

Lars was fed up with what he called the 'concrete layer', one level below him – the heads of business units who, he felt, defended their own interests and were impervious to change. He was sure many middle managers and front-line staff were receptive to being more innovative – but how to reach them?

Lars called in a leading international consulting firm. They analysed the problems and concluded that the company needed, from top to bottom, to learn to be more innovative. They recommended that the company adopt a new process for being innovative, based on international best practice. They set this out in a 250-slide PowerPoint presentation which was sent to subsidiaries around the world.

The impact? A mixture of embarrassment and indignation. Some experienced managers didn't know whether to laugh or cry. It was like 'painting by numbers', said one manager, 'the idea that you can make people develop great new products by following steps 1 to 60'.

Systems and processes

Information technology (IT) lends itself to the drive to improve quality and performance. We can do things much more quickly, and globally. It is much safer for doctors to prescribe drugs on a computer that can remind them of drug interactions and the patient's history. When we know that there is a *right* way to do something we can do it better and more consistently with the aid of technology. However, this same technology has enabled new, oppressive systems and processes in large organizations – banks, insurance and mobile phone companies, for example, which have teams and individuals all over the world working to a tight script.

To achieve a result, the teams must co-operate. Yet often they exist in carefully limited silos and don't have the authority or knowledge to respond effectively to customer needs. Technology, which in theory supports integration, in fact creates fragmentation, and organizations seem to have great difficulty securing internal cooperation or acting in a coordinated way to take opportunities or address problems. It's bonkers.

We run a local society and have a joint account with a well-known bank. To make payments to suppliers we need authorization by two directors of the society. We wanted to set up banking over the internet. We phoned the bank and were told that we should complete and return a form that would be sent to us in the post.

When the form arrived it was not the form we had been promised. We got back on the phone. We waded our way through multiple levels of 'You have four options'. After several calls, we were told that the first person we had spoken to 'had made a mistake' and that we would have to start again. We learnt that we had a 'relationship manager'. We asked for his phone number or email address but were told it was not possible to give us this information. He would phone us back. He never did. We heard that another form was on its way to us. When it arrived it also wasn't the form promised.

We complained and told our story to the bank's complaints department. After a few weeks a letter arrived, apologizing for the poor service and giving us cash compensation – but still no access to internet banking!

The problem seemed to be the way the bank was organized. Over several weeks we talked to a number of people, some apparently in the UK, some in India, some perhaps in the Far East. We had the impression that some really wanted to help, but always they needed to refer to another department in the bank or look up another file. They had a script to work to and could not go beyond it.

After six months – and hours on the phone – we despaired and decided to move our account to another bank. Will the service be better? Only time will tell.

Metrics mania and 'the radar'

Information on activity and performance is the lifeblood of modern organizations. It allows leaders to see the big picture – where things are going wrong or right. Information allows investors to make a judgement about an organization and its senior management. If you are an operational manager, information about the flow of the work you are managing is critical to your effectiveness. 'What gets measured gets managed' is axiomatic and measurement and 'metrics' are pervasive in organizational life. Some commercial companies communicate internally almost entirely by sharing metrics on everything that moves. In the public sector the concern to account for the use of public money leads to endless reviews and reports, which seem to those on the receiving end like a neurotic desire to check that a plant is growing by digging it up every few days and measuring its roots!

Metrics, performance data, the 'Balanced Scorecard' are a gift to senior management because they create a sense that 'we know what's going on' and can 'steer the ship' as a result. In commercial and public sector organizations people talk about being 'on the radar'. Or not, depending on your circumstances. Sometimes you want to be on the radar because it means you are being taken seriously. Sometimes you don't want to be on the radar because you will be punished.

We notice the gap in perspective between the 'Tops', 'Middles' and 'Bottoms' (as described by Barry Oshry) of organizations. What seems like essential 'performance management' at the top of organizations is experienced as oppressive, nonsensical and infantilizing among those in the front line. The Bottoms often feel distrusted and disrespected; they feel that their expertise and experience is of no account. The Middles often feel torn; they know the importance of hitting targets to satisfy the Tops, and they also know that it is not that simple because they see the Bottoms grappling with the inevitable contradictions and tensions that narrow targets create.

Faster communication

The internet and related technologies have transformed the way we communicate. They have supported globalization so that organizations can work around the clock. The speed of communication allows us to respond quickly and effectively to critical situations. We get early warning of potential difficulties that can be avoided. We know precisely where a product is, and when it will arrive, and can plan accordingly.

This too comes at a price. We know more, more quickly. Events that senior managers used to hear about after they had been resolved are immediately 'on the radar', raising anxiety and making it harder to judge what really needs your attention. Because we can communicate more widely more quickly, it is tempting to do so 'just in case', or in order to cover your back, with the result that situations that involve and could be resolved by two or three people are suddenly amplified. And you end up with a deluge of irrelevant messages to deal with. We find ourselves 'always on' – the electronic message in whatever form it arrives requires an immediate response. Superficially this can be exciting and provide us with a rush of serotonin, but as a consequence we become distracted in meetings or fail to allow ourselves uninterrupted thinking time to concentrate on something that really matters. And when do you sleep?

Are you 'aligned'?

Senior teams worry a lot about alignment, sometimes in relation to products and services, but more often in relation to people. Is what this group or individual does aligned with the strategy or the core business of this organization?

We assume that open debate and liberal democratic values are essential in society as a whole, yet suppress open discussion within organizations. Most people we meet are very cautious about saying what they really think to their boss. They don't want to be thought to be 'moaning' or, even worse, as someone who 'resists change'. The passion for organizational alignment suppresses expression of alternative perspectives. We live in a world of double-talk and double-think. Individuals get caught in the middle. Like Alice in Wonderland, they often feel bewildered and frightened. Sometimes they want to laugh their heads off; most of the time they keep their thoughts to themselves and conclude (like the proverbial Russian peasant) about the latest new initiative or edict from above, 'It'll pass.'

Unintended consequences

As organization consultants coming alongside people at all levels in organizations, what we often notice is the gap between intention and impact. Unintended consequences are everywhere.

We see many people in authority caught in patterns of behaviour that have an impact that is quite different from their apparent intention – humane, thoughtful leaders who do things that seem oppressive or infantilizing to those who work for or with them.

Restructuring, checklists, systems, metrics, rapid communication – all of which have their uses – seem to be running us, not the other way around. It's bonkers! Comprehensive appraisal processes, for example, are set up to hold people to account and develop them, but somewhere along the line the purpose gets lost, and the process becomes an elaborate paper exercise. Good intentions at the board level turn into something oppressive and infantilizing for those who do the work. How can we reconnect those in authority with those in the middle and on the front line?

Mary was a leading professor of public health in the UK whose work came to the attention of ministers because it seemed to shed light on some of the most serious health challenges facing the country. The government decided to finance a long-term £30 million research study led by Mary. It seemed like the proudest moment of Mary's career – for her work to be recognized by ministers and to secure such a large grant.

Two years later Mary was not so sure. What had seemed like a blessing was becoming a curse. 'I spend half my time writing reports, responding to strategy reviews and filling out risk registers. The level of scrutiny from government and its agencies is intense. When will I have time to get back to my research?'

How bonkers is that?

- Endless organizational upheavals – what we call 'Permanent Transition'. How are people supposed to give of their best, or form long-term partnerships, when they feel insecure and are constantly trying to work out what their role is and where they fit in with other individuals and groups?

- A preoccupation with plans and targets, form filling and box ticking that distorts people's priorities and drives out the real work that people are employed to do.

- Chief executives who say that their biggest problem is that they need more leaders at every level, but act in ways that kill leadership. Goffee and Jones say: 'They encourage either conformists or role players with an impoverished sense of who they are and what they stand for'.

- Information technology that in practice fosters fragmentation, disconnection and new oppressive, and maddening, forms of bureaucracy. This is not how IT was supposed to be.

- A mania for metrics as expressed by a partner in a Big Four consulting firm in 2015: 'If you can't measure it, it does not exist'. Competitive tendering processes that deny the importance of relationships and experience. Where has trust and judgement gone in all this?

- The 24–7 'always on' life. When are people able to pause and think about what is most important and how to achieve it?

- The call for alignment that ends up with people talking a 'management-speak', a language of pretence. Individuals are often afraid to speak, unable to tell their bosses what they really think and feel. How are people in authority supposed to learn what is really going on?

Normalizing the abnormal

The absurdities of corporate life have become a staple of TV comedy in programmes such as *The Office*. We often hear managers and leaders (in private moments) comment on the games and the pretence: 'Of course', they say, 'it is like that. What else do you expect?' The abnormal has become normal.

David Graeber, in his book *The Utopia of Rules*, suggests we are lost for words; we lack a way of talking about what we all live.

> 'Our lives have come to be organized around the filling out of forms. Yet the language we have to talk about these things is not just woefully inadequate – it might as well have been designed to make the problem worse. We need to find a way to talk about what is happening . . . to understand what is appealing about it, what sustains it, which elements carry within them some potential for redemption in a truly free society, which are best considered the inevitable price to pay for living in any complex society, and which can and should be entirely eliminated.'

So, is everything bonkers, or is it just me?

Disasters, like sporting metaphors, may not be a reliable guide to organizational life but can be illuminating.

On 8 January 1989, British Midland Flight 92, a Boeing 737-400, crashed onto the embankment of the M1 motorway near Kegworth in England. The aircraft was attempting to conduct an emergency landing at East Midlands Airport. Of the 126 people aboard, 47 died and 74, including seven members of the flight crew, sustained serious injuries.

The plane crashed because the pilots switched off the wrong engine. The left engine had a serious problem and the right was working normally. The pilots switched off the right engine because they thought that was the one with the problem. The passengers and crew in the cabin could see it was the left engine but assumed the pilots knew that so didn't tell them. The pilots couldn't see the engines and didn't ask their colleagues or the passengers.

Why tell this story now? Because it seems to us to be emblematic of today's organizations. Senior people operate separately from those they are serving, and rely heavily on technology and their own knowledge in isolation from others. Often the common-sense thing – looking out of the window in this case – doesn't happen. Those in the body of the organization (or plane) assume that those at the top (or front) know what they are doing and have the situation under control. It is not their place to say anything, with tragic consequences sometimes.

The heroic orthodoxy

These phenomena – the crazy call centres, the constant restructurings, the tick-box madness, the obsessive measurement, the 'management-speak' and the pretence, the fragmentation – do not arise by accident. They are part of a pattern.

They arise from the current orthodoxy about leadership and management, change and strategy, in organizations and business.

The orthodoxy is heroic. It centres on the need for transformational change to enable companies and organizations to adapt
and thrive in what is believed to be a period of unprecedented
change. The job of leaders, it is believed, is to drive through
change. Leaders need to have a clear vision, they need to persuade
others to 'buy in' and they need to show 'steely resolve' to realize
their vision when people 'resist change'. Change can and should
be 'managed'. These days, leaders need to show 'emotional intelligence' to handle the people and organizational issues, and be
skilled at 'engagement'. But still the picture persists of change
being done *to* organizations. Organizational culture is seen as the
enemy; it's difficult to shift, and the reason change efforts often
don't deliver the results required.

The orthodoxy is heroic at a number of levels. It assumes heroic
leaders, it requires heroic visions of how the organization (and
even the world) will be better, and it takes heroic resolve to realize
the vision.

The telltale signs of the heroic orthodoxy are the words and
phrases people use and take for granted: 'transformation', 'vision',
'driving change', 'resistance to change', 'incentives and penalties',
'management of change', 'risk', 'performance', 'relationships'
(and pretty well everything else), 'pace and scale', 'alignment',
'deliverables', 'gap analysis', 'metrics', 'engagement', 'buy-in'.

Like any orthodoxy, it is the set of beliefs people espouse in
order to be respectable, approved, conventional. To oppose the
orthodoxy is to risk being regarded as a heretic, beyond the pale;
someone who needs to be cast out. So people learn to speak the
heroic language and keep quiet about any doubts they may have.
This is a secular orthodoxy but, like religious orthodoxes, there is
an element of magic, or things that must be believed, whatever
reason or evidence says to the contrary.

The heroic orthodoxy shapes the assumptions and therefore
the actions of people in organizations. Like many paradigms
before, it is largely unseen. It is the sea in which we swim and
therefore goes unnoticed. It is 'just how things are'. And yet, as

with the normalizing of the abnormal, orthodoxy isn't necessarily 'right' – just accepted. What makes up the orthodoxy and how does it work? We say more in Chapter 2.

Indeed, there is a glaring contradiction at the heart of this orthodoxy. There is much talk of the need for 'transformational leadership', but the reality at the receiving end of the drive for change is *managerial* – a reliance on plans and targets, metrics and monitoring, form filling and box ticking.

The confusion about leadership and management is not only naïve and simplistic, it is in our view founded on a fundamental confusion about the roles of leadership and management in organizational life. The terms are used almost interchangeably with no appreciation of their difference.

Where has the orthodoxy come from, and how did it come to be so pervasive?

The heroic orthodoxy (see pages 91 and 92 and the Appendix for more details) has come from business schools and management consultancies over the past 40 years, and has spread into all areas of business and organizational life. Starting in the private sector, it has ridden the wave that 'business knows best', and triumphed now in public as well as in commercial organizations. Work in almost any business or organization nowadays and you will touch and feel this orthodoxy. With the help of IT there has been a convergence of private and public sectors. The private sector has become more bureaucratic and the public sector has aped the ways of business.

The orthodoxy has its roots in the Reagan/Thatcher revolution of the 1970s and 80s. The neo-liberals have a triumphant and compelling story to tell – we would all be freer, richer and better people if remaining obstacles to free markets, choice and competition were removed. 'Reform' and 'modernization' are code words that have come to mean more change towards the free market. What was said by Adam Smith (or at least part of it) in the 1770s was picked up by Hayek at the end of the Second World War and became triumphant after the collapse of Communism at the end of the 1980s. The neo-liberals feel vindicated by the remarkable transformation of China and many other developing societies.

Humans, it is argued, are economic animals who will respond to appropriate, rational incentives and penalties. Transformations are needed across society towards free markets. This requires powerful leadership from those at the top who understand this need, can persuade others to follow, and will show the determination to see the job through. Change is what it is all about. Those who dwell too long on the past (or are too concerned with the present) will fail to realize the wonderful future that is available. Leaders need to think through what change is needed and how they will achieve it, set this down in a clear strategy, and then have the courage to drive it through, whatever the obstacles.

Three other factors play a key role. One is IT and the internet revolution. Leaders can now aspire to sit in control rooms and call up on a screen every aspect of performance. They can construct 'Balanced Scorecards' which give them the illusion of control over their whole organization. Information technology has also led to chronic information overload; we have not yet learnt how to master the new technology but let ourselves be its servant.

Secondly, 'Big Data' fuelled by social media. The capacity of computers to handle Big Data has enabled significant scientific advances. As we are discovering, it also has a significant shadow side. Our personal data is much more public and accessible. It can be accessed and used for commercial and political purposes – with good or ill intent. These developments are not central to this book but they are changing the way we live and govern our societies. They are part of the landscape in today's organizations.

Thirdly, the development of 'machine bureaucracy', as Henry Mintzberg put it. This long predates the notion that 'markets know best' and the internet. All bureaucracies have a tendency to default to metrics and process. It has long been the job of leaders to push back from time to time and remind people of purpose, meaning and community. But in the current age, technology has enabled a new level of cack-handed systems and processes, of bureaucracy. There is no give in technology-enabled bureaucracy. You either comply or you don't. Yet, as we know, 'working to rule' ultimately leads to paralysis. There needs to be some flexibility, some human judgement in the application of all rules and procedures.

What has been remarkable has been the weakness of alternative narratives and the way that neo-liberal ideas have captured the political classes across the developed world. The neo-liberal agenda provides justification for those in the private sector and a compelling rationale for change in the public sector.

Any great idea, taken too far, can be destructive – even bonkers. What we find disturbing is the certainty of the champions of this neo-liberalism; their lack of interest in other perspectives; their lack of insight into the actual experience of implementing their ideas, and the obvious contradictions. True believers know what the answer is to any given problem. There is no need to enquire too deeply into issues, what the context is or what the problem really is. The remarkable achievements of freer markets are elevated into a panacea. Moving towards 'the market' is good; any move back from it is bad.

In a strange inversion, the neo-liberals have become the idealists, insisting that their idealized, fanciful picture be put into practice, whatever the obstacles. For what are pure free markets but a theoretical abstraction? The neo-liberals know that they are right. Where they can end up is smashing up institutions and cultures (see, for example, Andrew Lansley's 'reform' of the National Health Service (NHS) in the UK) in order to put their new order in place. In a dreadful parody of liberalism, they can become the 'Free Market Taliban'. We say more about this in the following chapters.

Sometimes it is just me, but mostly it's me and you and the context

We want to explore giving a different meaning to leadership and management, strategy and change.

We start in the next chapter by reclaiming the difference between leadership and management and, critically, by asserting the precedence of leadership over management. We do not want to denigrate management in its place as the servant of purposeful leaders, but we do claim that many of the absurdities, dysfunctions and terrors of modern organizational life stem from the managerial taking over from leadership. As a result we ignore our relationships, the social fabric which connects the organization; we denigrate our own experience and don't value the wonderful things that groups and organizations achieve; and we stop talking to each other about what matters because we are too busy with the email.

CHAPTER 2

It's a Mad World – Leadership and Management Turned Upside Down

In this chapter we argue for a fresh understanding of leadership and management, and of the relationship between the two. Both leadership and management are essential if organizations are to develop in sane, healthy ways. Leadership without management is vacuous and management without leadership is soul-destroying.

But we also suggest that management must be subordinate to leadership. This contrasts sharply with the heroic orthodoxy in which leadership, in the abstract, is seen as the answer to almost any problem but, in practice, the managerial approach is dominant – with serious and damaging consequences for individuals and organizations.

Leadership has become subordinate to management

How would you describe the difference between leadership and management? Are they different or interchangeable? The call for leadership, even transformational leadership, is loud in many organizations. At the same time there is a call for performance to be managed and directed towards measurable objectives and targets. Jobs and their related competencies are closely defined, protocols prescribed, procedures made systematic and in many cases handed over to computers to control.

It is as if some synthesis has occurred in the popular imagination so that leadership and management rest easily together. They are

29

complementary – 'both and' – but this is not an equal synthesis. Leadership has somehow become *subordinate* to management while being idealized as a magical and transforming object.

Leadership is seen as sexy. It requires us to be personally attractive, to draw others to follow us. Being recognized as a leader is something to aspire to. It is associated with more senior positions in organizations (directors are expected to be leaders) and more junior positions are described as managerial and supervisory. And yet, the managerial mentality dominates. How can this be so?

Management has triumphed over leadership because we can *grasp* it (more on the significance of the word *grasp* later). Management, it is said, defines, codifies, makes things systematic, predicts. Management is sure of itself and in control of the situation. Management spots variances and takes corrective action. You know where you are with management and, above all, we want to know where we are with our organizations. If I am a shareholder, I want to know what return to expect. If I am a customer, I want to know that I will get what I am paying for. If I am a patient, I want to know that my operation will go according to plan. If I am a venture capitalist, I want to know when the business will be ready to be sold profitably.

In other words, management is an imagined guarantee against the anxiety of losing control and being exposed to helplessness in the face of uncontrollable risks or events. Management is also a kind of insurance policy against the leader who is godlike, and for that very reason can't be trusted blindly.

So management is about *bringing order* to things. Leadership, on the other hand, is about *creating meaning* in groups and organizations. It is, we suggest, concerned with the shared and conflicting senses of purpose and of direction in groups. It involves discovering what is the priority and why. What are we seeking to achieve? And how do we build on the essence of what we have done before *and* create the new? Managers can direct, organize and control the work within their area of expertise and accountability; leaders deal with the boundary issues and build bridges between departmental silos, providing cohesion in an organization.

Today's organizations kill leadership

Powerful people often call for leadership, while in practice preventing it from emerging. As Goffee and Jones point out:

'When we ask CEOs what's the biggest problem they face they unerringly reply: our organization needs more leaders at every level . . . organizations desire leaders but structure themselves in ways that kill leadership. Far too often, our organizations – in business, in the public sector and in the not-for-profit sector – are machines for the destruction of leadership. They encourage either conformists or role players with an impoverished sense of who they are and what they stand for.'

For people who don't fit with the prevailing norms there is a double whammy. As Meyerson and Scully describe:

'They challenge the status quo, both through their intentional acts and also just by being who they are, people who do not fit perfectly . . . both the professional and personal identities are strong and salient; they do not appear alternately for special situations. In most situations, the pull of each identity only makes the opposite identity all the more apparent, threatened and painful.'

Recognizing interdependence

Leadership is concerned with the collective. It involves recognition that you are dependent on others; this is not some deficit on your part; it allows you to respect the experience and skills of those whom you need to engage in a joint enterprise. The others sense your willingness to enquire, connect and develop some intention together. They can then attach to you and the shared direction and task.

This sense of interdependence matters to us as human beings – to connect to others and to some purpose and meaning is part of what it means to be human.

We constantly strive to make sense of the world. However, this is often deeply uncomfortable in organizational life. It leads to 'awkward' questions. It may challenge the status quo and, most threateningly, the power structure.

When people lead well (we suggest) they acknowledge different interests and viewpoints. They recognize *not* knowing and having faith; trusting others and trusting 'your self'.

And uncertainty

Leadership highlights uncertainty – the things we cannot know and cannot control. It is rooted in previous experience and based on intuition and subjective judgement. However, uncertainty is inimical to modern organizational life; risk management procedures and quality control aim to eliminate it from working life.

As a result of this mindset the idea of leadership has been reduced to the functional and utilitarian in order to direct followers towards prescribed managerial goals and objectives. Leadership has been redefined by stealth. This may not have been intentional. Just as the colours in a picture hanging on a wall may fade unnoticed over time, so our understanding of leadership has faded and with it our sense of what it means to be human at work, and not just at home.

The danger of putting abstract ideas ahead of experience

In his book *The Master and his Emissary*, Iain McGilchrist explores the relationship between the left and right hemispheres of the brain and the effect of that relationship on the history of the western world. His central contention is that the 'Master' (right hemisphere) has been usurped by the 'Emissary' (left hemisphere), and this parallels the subordination of leadership to management. The left hemisphere 'controls' the right hand and, for most of us, it is with the right hand that we grasp the world, and this is enormously useful to us. It gets things done but what happens if it takes over? In his concluding chapter McGilchrist speculates about what a world dominated by the left hemisphere would look like. Sound familiar?

- Abstraction: 'the substitution of information and information gathering, for knowledge which comes through experience' . . . 'more and more work would come to be overtaken by the meta process of documenting or justifying what one was doing or supposed to be doing – at the expense of the real job in the living world' . . . 'there is a complete loss of the sense of uniqueness'.

- Reification or modelling the real world on the mechanical: 'when we deal with a machine there are three things we want to know: how much can it do, how fast can it do it, and with what degree of precision' . . . 'Numbers, which the left hemisphere feels familiar with and is excellent at manipulating (though it may be remembered is less good at understanding what they mean), would come to replace the response to individuals, whether people, places things or circumstances which the right hemisphere would have distinguished. "Either/or" would tend to be substituted for matters of degree and a certain inflexibility would result' . . . 'In human affairs, increasing the amount or extent of something, or the speed with which something happens, or the inflexible precision with which it is conceived or applied, can actually destroy' . . . 'The right hemisphere's appreciation of How (quality) would be lost.'

Abstraction and reification feature in most debates about public policy. For example, is the primary purpose of schools and education the achievement of examination results? Is the only thing that matters to the stock market the short-term return to shareholders? Is the purpose of healthcare to eliminate illness and prolong life at all costs? In all of these cases, if the answer to the question is 'yes' then leadership has become subordinate to management. We have lost sight of purpose, context, meaning and relationship in favour of the graspable, measurable and concrete. It's not only 'what gets measured gets managed' but also 'what matters is what's measurable'. In the end what we measure then takes over and manages us.

Of course, we are aware that the analogy with the left and right brain hemispheres is individualistic and does not amount to a comprehensive explanation of what goes on at a collective level. Suffice to say that the goal-driven carrot and stick culture spreads fear at all levels of the organization, and people tend to focus on covering their backs by getting their facts and figures right.

Leadership as getting people to do what you want

It may not have been intended, but our faded understanding of leadership is a consequence, paradoxically, of the 'leadership industry' and the dominance of micro-management, on the back of computerized accountability. The question 'What kind of people do we have and what can they do?' is displaced by the question 'What is in the business plan and in the strategy document?' Subsequently the question is 'How can the plan, the strategy, the objectives and the people be aligned?'

Leadership becomes 'getting people to do what the top leader, the abstract plan and the administrative system want them to do' in order to satisfy the performance measures, the bonus targets.

Leadership is charged with sweetening and softening the bitter pill of change. Participative processes and consultation exercises

34

become a way of cajoling people into doing things differently through the illusion of being involved in some way. Leadership itself is reduced to a trainable set of competencies. In recent times leaders have been required to become 'emotionally intelligent'. The assumption is that a leader who matches the competencies will, as night follows day, be successful in leading – or more accurately, engineering desired changes in performance. 'Leading change' comes to mean managing change. It is defined as moving from the current unsatisfactory order of things to a prescribed future order.

All these approaches put (albeit unconsciously) management before leadership. It is assumed that change can be lived through in predictable steps; in an orderly fashion. We have experienced that designed change processes founder time and time again. The only thing that does seem predictable is the failure of engineered change from the top, without involvement of all levels of the organization.

One of the reasons is that we mistake management for leadership and avoid the risk involved in all change, all human interaction and communication. The other reason is that emotions are really not intelligent; they are emotional and subjective and therefore have a non-mechanistic and intuitive logic to them.

It is the subjective, emotional aspect of the interaction between leader, organizational neighbours and customers that is the target of managerial planners, strategists and controllers. Management believes in the magic power of systems, rules and technological and mathematical processes of evaluation and measurement. Leaders depend on the subconscious power of human intuition and knowledge of what people can accomplish together when they relate, interact and turn away from control to play, imagination and creation through trial and error and experimentation.

The value of good management

One of the ironies of the managerial orthodoxy is that it has in many places given management a bad name. In universities and the NHS, in many large corporations, in government and elsewhere, people experience a *managerial* approach with excessive planning and control, metrics mania, tick-box madness and the other phenomena described in Chapter 1. They lose sight of high-quality management and how essential it is – the sort of management that gets things done and delivers essential services. Organizations need good management.

Our advanced understanding of how to 'bring order' and control to things has radically changed our world, making us safer, wealthier and healthier. Of course, that statement is only credible if qualified by the statement 'to some extent', because it is also possible to argue that technology (which is central to our ability to 'bring order') has made us less safe, less healthy and poorer. In other words, we need to understand the world as a whole and to see things in their context, which highlights the fundamental error in subordinating leadership to management.

To manage well requires us to take a narrow focus on a specific, measurable objective. In other words, to *de*-contextualize, to only consider those variables that can be affected in some way and certainly not to dwell too much on the meaning of what we are seeking to achieve or its likely wider consequences. How many management meetings have you been in where frustration grows with the individual who insists on raising 'irrelevant' questions, usually a question which is seeking to *widen* the context of the discussion? Disciplined, narrow, detailed management conversations are very necessary and useful in organizational life. However, if our understanding of leadership is limited to persuading or cajoling people to have the management conversation that we as leader have predetermined, then that's bonkers!

On 'getting a grip'

One of us worked for a regional CEO within a global corporation. He was a demanding and exciting boss. You had to be on your mettle, and above all else, do what you said you were going to do otherwise you would not be trusted. You could renegotiate what you said you would do if there was good reason, but 'not delivering' was a cardinal sin. The CEO was strongly attached to the idea of 'grip' and expected the CEOs of the many organizations that reported to him to 'have a grip'. This meant knowing what was going on in your organization, and more critically, taking responsibility for what was happening. There were (at least) two ways to really upset this man. First, by knowing less than he did about what was going on in your organization (easier than it sounds because his grasp of the figures was impressive and he was very well connected). Secondly, by talking about what was going on as if you were a spectator and not someone with a sense of responsibility for what was happening, particularly if things were going wrong.

Management knows the data in the same way as the scorer at a sporting event keeps track of things. Knowing the score as a leader is necessary, but far from sufficient. Leaders also need a deep understanding of their part in creating that score – however tough that is to recognize. This man embodied both ways of knowing.

An unexceptional story of transformational change

As we explore in the next chapter, the heroic orthodoxy is obsessed with change that is transformational. The next story illuminates what happens to the relationship between leadership and management when change is expected to be transformational.

The story is set some years ago in a large NHS hospital and begins with politicians and policy makers finding that healthcare organizations in the United States had much more advanced computer technology. There was an obvious reason for this. From its very beginnings the US healthcare system had been insurance-based, so all activity for each patient had to be recorded in order to create a bill. The history and foundations of the NHS are quite different; nonetheless it seemed obvious that the NHS could make much better use of computers and so the government of the day initiated some pilot projects. Most took the approach of buying and adapting a US system, but some took a different approach. The aim in this example was to design a brand new system around the patient using the latest technology. The management information, such as the cost of a patient's treatment that was the raison d'être of the US systems, would be a by-product of a fully integrated system through which all activity was conducted. This was an honourable goal, and potentially transformational.

As is usual, the business case was constructed. The vision described included radically different 'transformed' health services, made more efficient and safer. Quantifiable benefits were identified showing how the system would pay for itself over a reasonable period of time. There had to be a strong business case because of the level of investment required. Experts were called in to analyse and plan; to produce the cost–benefit equation in order to make sure it was worth it and to outline the sequential steps to arrive at the transformation. After much scrutiny and delay, the project was funded. A team was constructed to develop the IT system comprising hospital staff and the chosen supplier. Another supplier was contracted to deliver 'change management' once the system was built.

The project team was housed (along with the computers that needed a secure home) in a remote part of the hospital campus. The IT supplier's expensive cars were parked outside and the team were quickly described as 'overpaid and over there', in other words, 'nothing to do with us'. The third party contracted to provide 'change management' (no mention of leadership) showed up with various tools for measuring 'commitment' and 'resistance' amongst other things. It was impertinent to mention the threat to jobs.

After 18 months or so the plan was to pilot the first phase of implementation and for change management to begin. However, there had been multiple problems developing the IT, most of which had been hidden until this point. A lot of money had been spent and the politics of the situation required that there could be no scandal. This is not unique to the public sector of course; politics whether spelt with a large or small 'p' trumps the business case every time.

There were many immediate, serious problems to address. At first there were sackings and redundancies to control costs alongside an internal process of 'tell us everything you know that is wrong'. Those leading the attempted recovery had to lead as if something could be made of the project, knowing that this was highly uncertain. By being part of carrying on they were also part of a political decision. The price of 'pulling the plug' was too high, not only because of the ensuing political scandal but also because the fallout would have damaged the running of a good hospital. There had to be compromise and accommodation that included all the principal parties, including the supplier.

After the initial trauma of redundancies and restructuring had passed, the new project management team could examine what had happened to the transformation. On some of the more straightforward parts of the system the team discovered that people on the wards and in the offices were ahead of them. They had got fed up waiting for the long-promised clever system to arrive and had begun to use what they had to address their immediate problems. For example, they found they didn't need a sophisticated ordering system to significantly improve the lives and efficiency of the porters. Emailing a request for a porter to a central mailbox was much quicker for nurses than queuing on the phone, and the porters were able to organize their work much more sensibly. It was also relatively straightforward to create an ordering system that was even better and could be used by many more services. Of course today this technology is unremarkable; but this was a number of years ago.

This story is not primarily about process improvement supported by technology, although the efficiency of transactions was indeed significantly improved and money was saved. More importantly, patients had a more reliable service, and nurses and porters slightly less hassle. Even more importantly in terms of transformation, nurses, porters and their leaders had a story to tell together to the hospital board. In the middle of the organizational bonkers they had created something together and their relationship had changed.

Despite everything, imaginative staff had found utility in the IT. Although many thought the whole project should have been abandoned, some retained sufficient enthusiasm. For several years the team persisted with this incremental approach and in time implemented much of what had been intended, albeit with a different technical strategy. The cost–benefit analysis found that in many ways the system paid for itself, but not in ways that had been in the original plan. Over the years the recovered IT system became the bedrock of an advanced and successful information strategy, albeit in ways different from those first envisaged. Turns out the political decision to continue may not have been a bad one.

However, if you audit the business case it would not have been worth it because all that counts is the extent to which you have done what you said you would do in the first place. Creative adaptation and inventive ways of using something for additional purpose, however much they make a difference, don't count. The logic of the original business case is inescapable. The usual response when things have not worked out according to the plan is not to query the methodology but to call for greater precision in using this method in the future, as if more detail makes predicting the future more certain.

What can we make of this story?

This story is characterized as 'unexceptional' because our expectation is that you will recognize your own experience. Transformational change is announced, heralded as truly different, a long time in advance. Then, quite often, it seems to go away and is forgotten about by those it is intended to affect, except for a few people on the project team who continue to beaver away. Then the transformation reappears, but not quite as you remember it, and it is not that brilliant; in fact it is quite ordinary. Then there might be a bit of a fuss about what has happened with some mutual recrimination. Then it goes quiet and the transformation is not spoken about; but some quite useful things live on and the world is different in some small but significant ways.

It is easy for our common experience of transformation to make us cynical, and many have written about the phenomenon of 'change fatigue' in modern organizational life. In many ways the cynical response is the most attractive because it frees us of responsibility. Transformation is something that 'they' do and it has nothing to do with us. Except of course, it does. If you are involved in organizational life, and in particular carrying some responsibility for leadership and management, how you respond matters. There were many well-paid expert consultants involved in the recovery of the IT system, but one of the most significant contributions came from those porters and nurses who found a way to make it useful to them. This is an example of local leadership *and* management in action that provides a foundation for wider recovery.

At the heart of the story was a radical, transformational idea. The big idea was that whether you are ordering a sandwich or a blood test, the process involved is the same. An appropriately authorized person places the order, others act on it, and there is a clear end to the process once the results have been delivered. Sounds obvious, straightforward even, and it seemed to the analysts at the time that new forms of database technology made it possible to build an operational system using these principles. Turns out they were wrong and it was much harder than anticipated. So, as a leader, what might you conclude from this? Never work with children, animals or IT? Never have a big idea, don't be too ambitious?

To say 'they were wrong' presents the world in black and white terms. It encourages us to think that the idea itself was 'wrong', the analysts mistaken and that nothing else matters. It would be more accurate to say that this was a failed experiment rather than a failed idea; and at the heart of the failure is the splitting of leadership and management – something that the very idea of transformational change (as commonly constructed) invites.

In this construction, leadership is conceived as vision – being able to see beyond the present in a necessarily abstract way. In feeding our abstract vision we become drawn to idealization – what might be possible in a perfect world? So our vision gathers momentum and we become more excited and attached to the possibility. At the same time, we turn a blind eye to our knowledge of the likelihood that ideals can be more of a fantasy than a translatable and realistic course of action.

Leadership and the social process of taking initiative with and through others is already in danger of becoming abstracted and detached – belonging only to those who can 'see' and know better than others. It is at this moment of disconnection that an ideal vision of how things should be becomes potentially destructive for those who hold the intent. At this juncture they put the plan before their relationship with the people who have to implement it and make it all work. After the split the leaders own the plan and the managers own the translation of it into reality. This split creates a three-class society in the organization – the god-like idealists at the top, the threatening and frightened managers in the middle, and the objects of the plan at the bottom. The emotional attachment of the front-line staff to the leader and the visionary plan is severed and the change process is sabotaged by its own design. Even more importantly, the knowledge that people work for people, not for plans on paper, gets lost and the plan turns into a sacred object with a life of its own. The plan becomes the subject, the people its object.

Most humans like it the other way round, and if this need was respected more, leaders and managers could team up and work together and could get real about needing help from the people they are asking to change.

In the transformational construction of change the next step is the creation of the business case, which belongs firmly in the world of management – bringing order to things. This takes us down the path of describing radically different, 'transformed' businesses involving a massive increase in sales, customer satisfaction, service quality – or whatever the measures happen to be, so long as there are quantifiable measures and targets, many of which must be financial. In other words, there must be a strong business case for the change because significant investment is sure to be required. If there is to be significant investment, then there must be control in the form of project and programme management to ensure the benefits are delivered. In order to justify the investment it seems inevitable that costs will be underestimated and benefits overestimated.

Moreover, to allay the anxiety of investment, specific detail is required. For example, it was predicted this transformational IT system would save each and every nurse half an hour of administrative time on each and every shift. There were a lot of nurses, and if you multiplied the number of nurses by the half-hour savings (which the business case did) you could manage with many fewer of them, saving lots of money and recovering more than the costs of the system. If you think about health services from the perspective of day-to-day activity on a busy ward, with teams of staff who treat and care and respond to events, then this reductionist approach is nonsense. Where is this spare half an hour? The (management) business case has also become abstracted and decontextualized.

Implementing IT systems in the complex world of healthcare is notoriously difficult, and there have been many failures and compromises. Perhaps the world of IT programmes is the place of greatest need for 'holding it all together', and the place where it is least likely to happen. Leadership and management collapse into their separate, respective idealized, abstracted and reduced forms. We lose sight of their difference and separate importance, and leadership is subordinated to the more graspable management. That's bonkers!

What could have been done differently?

With hindsight, there was another way to think about what was happening – and an alternative way of acting. As the eighteenth-century politician and philosopher Edmund Burke would have anticipated (see Chapter 3), there was wisdom in the organization, in accumulated practice and experience, which was valuable but not tapped in to. It was arrogant for senior managers and expert consultants to deny the value of others and think that only they could understand the needs and plan solutions.

From our perspective, it is better to rely on people at all levels from the start and involve them in considering what the organization could look like.

In this case, the hospital porters and the nurses became the strategic actors. It was they who triggered the development that was useful and sustained. How often have we experienced this in our work with organizations! In doctors' surgeries it is often receptionists who have the clearest experience of how the work actually gets done, and who are crucial to any development of systems and ways of working. In factories it is workers on the shop floor, in financial services firms it is sales people and administrative staff. When change occurs, it is often achieved through people close to the front line responding to immediate needs and pressures.

The job of those with authority is then to stop obsessing about what staff *should* be doing with the planned transformation and observe what they *are actually* doing. They should work with how the plan is actually being used, rather than striving to enforce its use. They will often discover the transformative effect of the initiative or change, only it's not exactly the transformation intended.

How do you put the equivalent of your porters and nurses at the centre of the picture?

Finding a workable relationship between leadership and management

A few years ago we worked with one of the world's leading cancer research centres. It does brilliant work, at the forefront of science and clinical practice. We were asked (unusually) to undertake a review of its management processes.

What we found, at first, seemed in some ways a bit of a mess. The management group met monthly and seemed much too big – more than 20 people crammed into a small downstairs room. Very busy people were involved and came and went at different points in meetings. The director of the centre took periods of the meeting to 'grandstand', talking about the important people around the world whom he had met recently and what they had discussed. He also broadcast information on the latest changes in Department of Health policy and practice. It was not clear what others in the meeting could contribute. Some people were silent throughout.

The director of the centre was a clinician and scientist and the lead manager was called the Secretary. All very old-fashioned. No chief executive. Some leading figures were very critical (privately) of the management processes. There was a call for stronger leadership. One person told us in confidence: 'The director is a scientist and he just does not understand leadership or management. He does not realize his job is to have the vision, persuade everyone that this is the right vision for us and then show "steely resolve" to push his vision through. Instead he wastes time on small stuff like drafting and redrafting the annual report. He does not realize what his priorities should be. The director handles non-executive directors badly. He wants to share problems with them – which they find alarming – rather than giving them a sense of purposeful action to find solutions.'

Yet, as we talked with people across the centre, we came to a very different conclusion. Yes, the director did sometimes micro-manage. Yes, he could handle non-execs more sensibly. He could be more adaptable and think about when he needed to be in executive mode as opposed to scientific researcher mode. All that seemed true.

But there was another side to what the director and secretary (and others) had developed together over the years. There was a remarkable ethos in the centre. No one doubted that the organization existed to improve health and patient care, to find therapies to prevent or reduce appalling suffering. Many of the managers and directors of the centre had loved ones and relatives who had been lost to cancer. Linked to this, the centre was able to recruit very high-calibre people. Some staff had formerly earned much more in the City, but were happy to work at the centre. What's more, the science came first. From the secretary down, managers offered comments and suggestions – not to block the science but to help make it happen. We saw sharp disagreements when managers pointed to financial, human resource or other constraints that seemed to block the scientists from doing what they wanted. The managers expressed in simple and clear terms the practical implications of rules that the centre had to live with. But in the end, it was always clear that the managers were trying to help; to enable the science and not block it.

The acid test was IT (it often is!). The centre had very capable IT managers who worked hard to deliver workable IT solutions to scientists who were very demanding. The IT managers had a reputation for being 'can-do' and pragmatic. They were not the butt of constant criticism, as they are in so many organizations, caught between the great promise of IT and a dismal reality.

What the Institute had discovered, after many years of trial and error, was a way of working in which leadership – what we are here for, the purpose of the organization – came first, and high-quality management worked hard to support the purpose and direction set by the scientific leadership. It turned out that the director and secretary had had some sharp disagreements over the years. They still had their tensions but had negotiated a working arrangement which now served them well. From time to time in management meetings the director would turn to the secretary and ask: 'Can we do that?' or 'What do we need to do to achieve our objective?' The secretary would respond with some pragmatic and doable suggestions.

For all the imperfections, the Institute has developed a culture where leadership comes first and management comes close behind to provide what the organization needs.

And now for another story.

Gaming, deception and integrity

Alan, a senior director in financial services, arrives troubled for his coaching meeting. A problem has come to light in his business unit. The manager submitting the monthly return to HQ has been manipulating the figures. Data on several hundred customers has been missed out. This manager does not report to Alan and what he reports is not part of Alan's responsibility. However, the CEO knows that Alan can be trusted in a crisis and so he asks him to sort it out. Alan is angry. He thinks the manager should be sacked and that they should 'come clean' to HQ. His boss takes a different view. He thinks that 'coming clean' will mean that they will be sacked too. The problem is not so large that it cannot be papered over.

Alan does what he is told, and through a painstaking process and sleepless nights over several months, the problem is solved, without damaging any customers. Nonetheless, Alan feels he is implicated and complicit, compromised in his relationship with his boss, which suffers.

There is a risk of taking this chapter to mean we are splitting the world into bad management and good leadership; but that is not our intention. Rather, we want to highlight the dangers to organizational integrity if we do not hold leadership and management together – interdependent. In his kinder moments Alan was prepared to accept that the manager who created the problem didn't mean to. Possibly, on a bad day, towards the end of a month when the report was due, this manager had spotted one or two customers who had been missed. He knew the consequences of 'owning up' to this and so chose to hide it. You can see that this is a familiar story akin to taking some cash from the till with the intention of putting it back. We don't know if this was the case in this specific example, but our experience of things going wrong in organizational life is that this is how they start, usually.

As soon as a metric or target is announced the arguments about definition begin and the fine lines between accurate reporting and gaming are explored. Once gaming extends to covering up, the position becomes impossible. It is at that precise moment when the integrity in the relationship between leadership and management is broken.

Management, measurement, grip or grasp is vital in the running of complex organizations. Once you have compromised the data you have begun to lose track of what is happening in your organization. To know the significance of management is itself an act of leadership. Measured by its own lights, management is free to manipulate the data because the only thing that really matters is that the numbers add up in their own terms. Management does not have to worry that each data point represents a customer, or someone to be made homeless when their house is repossessed. Management is only interested in the immediate result.

For organizations to function with integrity, management must be subordinate to leadership because leadership pays attention to context, purpose and meaning. If in that moment the manager had acted as a leader, and had had the necessary conversations, there is every prospect that the world would have been a better and more forgiving place. To get to this point it is necessary for leaders to re-learn that human cultural organizations always involve a degree of make-believe, if only by denying how much intuitive knowledge we each bring to a situation where we are asked to do something, engage in dialogue or deliver on targets we know are unrealistic.

Often the first casualty of the subordination of leadership to management is our own sense of integrity. Most obviously in Alan's story he became complicit in a cover-up. This example carries the added anxiety of public exposure and it also serves to remind us that leaders often face agonizing choices. Alan's business was well run by a competent CEO and leadership team. Their dismissal by a harsh and unforgiving performance management regime would have damaged the organization, perhaps much more significantly. Containing, or covering up, may have been the moral course of action. In Chapter 5, 'The Settled (Enough) Self', we explore further the ways in which we are stretched as a leader.

There is of course no one thing called 'leadership', and no one thing called 'management'. Both are subjective activities, not objects. We sometimes lead and we sometimes manage, and we do so in thousands of different ways, depending on the moment and the context. In this chapter we have challenged the muddled thinking that holds 'them' as interchangeable while subordinating leadership to management. We want to value the distinctive contribution of both, and more fundamentally, the integrity or wholeness of holding both together in a dynamic relationship – mentally as well as practically.

If you want to lead, ask yourself in critical moments:

- Is this something I should delegate and have managed by others?

- What kind of involvement do the managers need from me?

- What do I need to hear that they are saying?

- Do the managers need me to get out of the way?

- Is this more fundamental and strategic and I need to bring together the key people and think with them about the best way forward?

In the next chapter we explore the second pillar of the current heroic orthodoxy – the relentless call for transformational change.

CHAPTER 3

Addicted to Change – How We've Become Change Junkies

'Change, it's the only sign of life' – as the ageing Sebastian reflects in Evelyn Waugh's *Brideshead Revisited*. We cannot stand still, we are impelled towards the future; it's human. So too in organizational life *change* is the mantra. We have become addicted to change.

Since the second half of the twentieth century a language has been created – supported by business schools and consultancies around the world – to describe the orthodoxy of organizational change. Essential terms are 'vision', 'mission', 'strategy', 'strong leadership' and 'a burning platform'.

It is said we live in a time of unprecedented change. There is much talk of how technological and technical change is happening faster and faster. To keep up, organizations also need to change rapidly.

Most people, it is assumed, resist change. They hang on to existing ideas and practices. Leaders must be prepared to insist and impose their will. Their primary job is to bring about the change that is needed if the organization is to adapt and survive in a time of ever-increasing change in the world.

Organizational culture is said to be particularly resistant to change, stubbornly impervious. In order to shift engrained patterns of thinking and behaviour, leaders must shock and disturb their organizations; they must shake them out of their natural complacency and inward-looking tendencies.

In this thinking we set senior leaders apart from their organization. The assumption is that leaders need to know the answer

– where their company or organization should go, what it needs to look like in three to five years – and have the resolve to lead people there.

In the current orthodoxy, leaders need to communicate and sell the vision to staff and to key outsiders. Leaders also need to produce a strategy, a high-level statement of goals and ways to reach them; a plan for bridging the gap between where the organization is now and where it needs to be in the future. Strategy is for the few at the top of organizations. Only they have the intellect, breadth of perspective and the concern for corporate good that is required.

Of course, you need balls (a strong will), a big brain and great insight into your industry in order to work all this out. An enormous amount rests on the shoulders of the chief executive who is the most important person in the organization. A super-effective chief executive is absolutely necessary; you can't start without them, and you must accept that you will have to pay the (considerable) going rate, and make sure they have real incentives to stick around.

Once the strategy is agreed it can be turned into business objectives that can be made local, personal and (critically) measurable so that performance can be managed and rewarded; there must be incentives to support the 'SMART' objectives! With all this apparatus in place, leaders can lead and managers can manage.

Behind the leaders come the managers whose job is to 'deliver' the chosen direction. Once the plans are set the work is to implement the plan as fully as possible, to ensure that everyone is 'aligned'. 'Whingeing' about the difficulties of implementation is not welcome; staff need to focus on solutions not problems. The vision for the future of the organization should shape all their actions and decisions, not backward-looking concerns for past glories or current difficulties.

The leader will inevitably be a solitary hero, carrying the heavy responsibility of guiding the organization as a whole and seeing the bigger picture of what is needed. They will carry the burden of having to judge who in the company has the capability to do what is needed. The leader must be calm, thoughtful and resolute. Leaders need to stick with the vision and strategy when the going gets tough – as it inevitably will. By accepting their role as the originators and owners of the plan for the future, leaders volunteer (albeit subconsciously) to become the embodiment of success – and set themselves up as the potential scapegoat, should things turn out differently. Heroic leaders sense the potential insecurity of their position and delegate the responsibility of making the grand plan work (also subconsciously) to their deputies and middle managers, who for this reason often feel unsure of what they are meant to do.

Spend any length of time in any organization and you will touch and feel this orthodoxy and its attendant ways of doing things. Middle managers will bemoan the lack of a clear enough vision and worry about getting sufficient commitment from their teams. They will be on the lookout for the inevitable resistance to change and know that some people will take a lot of persuading before they 'buy in'.

In recent years the image of leader as solitary hero has softened. There is evidence that more emphasis is now put on skills of engagement, on the question 'How do you get your people to 'buy in' to your vision and strategy?' Yet the essential picture of heroic leadership, change and strategy remains the same as before.

This orthodoxy is associated with the success of hugely profitable businesses with Gross Domestic Product (GDP) larger than those of many countries. This has drawn the attention of governments, many of which have adopted the orthodoxy in the public sector.

Whether we are aware of it or not, this orthodoxy has an iron grip on the thinking and actions of most leaders of organizations. It has become the sea that we swim in and are not aware of – and it's largely bonkers!

A former CEO of a FTSE 100 company and chairman of a large public sector organization was talking at a board meeting of an organization of which he is a non-executive director: 'My job was to drive through change. Middle managers and staff won't understand at first; you have to get them out of their comfort zones. Eventually, those that can will get it.'

Here is a story of one would-be transformational leader who sought to drive cultural and other organizational change.

Driving change

Simon was the new managing partner of a national UK law firm that had formed as a result of a series of mergers of regional firms over 10 years. In his late forties, Simon was an unusual lawyer. He was a radical and a visionary. Early in his career he had had a spell working in the legal department of a large corporate client. It left a permanent mark. He was impatient of traditional legal ways of working. He kept asking why processes took so long. He was very focused on value for the client and commercial realities. His interest was in using the law to help clients achieve their objectives.

Simon could be engaging, outgoing and often quite direct in his comments and thoughts. Some people warmed to his directness; others were offended by some of his off-hand remarks. Yet people who got to know Simon felt that there was a lot going on that he did not share. Clearly he was a very driven individual. He had not done well at university but focused on sport and social life. He did not come from a privileged background – unlike many of his colleagues. In sport as a young man, and now at work, he was determined to win; to prove that he was as good as those who started life with a 'silver spoon in their mouths'. He was passionate about modernizing the firm. A recent episode had also touched a nerve – a complaint against Simon by a difficult client was still making its way through a seemingly endless Law Society process.

54

Simon worked for a charismatic older senior partner who had led the mergers and who had a distinctive vision of the new firm serving small- and medium-sized businesses across the country. The senior partner was now very busy with a role he had taken leading an international alliance of lawyers.

After several months of induction, of meeting partners and staff around the country, Simon wondered how he should proceed. He was clear that he had a mandate for change. The senior partner wanted much more of a 'One Firm' approach – a way of working and serving clients that was the same whether the client was in Newcastle or Northampton, Solihull or Stevenage. There was a lot more business to be won, Simon was convinced, if there was more of a common approach and if the firm was more joined up. It was crazy that clients came to the firm for only part of their legal needs. The firm should be a full service provider.

But how to lead the change? The local lead partners were well entrenched. They were in position because they had been success-ful locally. They had strong personal links to the senior partner, built up over a decade of building the firm together. Simon felt he could not challenge local autonomy directly. He decided to engage one of the Big Four consulting firms to examine how to modern-ize working processes in the firm.

After a few months the consulting firm produced their report. It was everything Simon had hoped for. It highlighted the differ-ences in working processes across the firm and the contradictions and confusions in structures and reporting lines. It estimated that big savings were possible if the firm centralized back-office processes, and identified a big potential for growth if marketing was both centralized and run on a more professional basis.

Simon sought the reactions of the senior partner and those close to him. Throughout his time with the firm he was always very careful to keep in close touch with the senior hierarchy. He sought out the senior partner, who was often travelling abroad, and secured a regular private dinner with him. Simon seemed to *have a knack for staying in tune with the preoccupations and concerns of senior figures, and proposing courses of action that seemed to meet their needs.*

After some months of discussion Simon came up with a radical new structure. There would be one national firm. The local lead partner roles would be abolished and local offices would report to a new central office in London. A central team would take on responsibility for national marketing, standard setting and co-ordination.

Local lead partners were, not surprisingly, up in arms. They protested to the national senior partner. However, Simon had clearly judged the senior group well. In the 18 months Simon had been with the firm the mood at the top had changed. Enough of moving slowly, slowly, it was said. If a proper national firm was to be built, 'some eggs might need to be broken'.

And, at the same time, the senior partner insisted Simon hold a series of facilitated meetings with local lead partners. Could genuine common ground be found? The senior partner said it was important to 'take the local lead partners with us'.

The meetings were inconclusive. Simon promised to 'take on board' the comments made by local partners. In conversation he was very conciliatory. However, over time local partners felt their views were ignored. Apart from delaying changes by over a year, it was not clear what effect the consultation had had.

Many people felt that Simon had gone through the motions of being seen to consult, but that he had not really engaged. They experienced Simon as appearing to be open when he spoke with them, but not saying what he really thought. A gap opened up between what people thought he was doing and how he presented himself.

It seemed that Simon was not prepared to talk to the local practice leaders openly about his full intentions. He wanted to develop a firm focused on client service and contribution to client businesses. Yet when he was with local practice leaders he seemed unable to articulate his passion. He came over as strangely hesitant. Some people began to believe that he was disguising his real intentions. It was maddening.

Part of the difficulty was that Simon delegated all aspects of implementation to a group of his staff who were frequently criticized. Simon was a good delegator. Local partners could not tell if the implementation group was implementing Simon's wishes – or being incompetent.

We got to know two middle managers who were tasked with implementing the new organization. Both were women – effective managers, dedicated to the success of the firm and trying their best to do a good job. It was striking how costly the process was for them. They looked very unhappy in their new roles. We had the sense that they were forced to 'choose sides' between the old regime and Simon's team. They felt close to people on both sides but opted for those in authority. They seemed to feel shame at 'betraying' those they had worked with closely. They were experienced as inauthentic. When confronted by the questions and confusions of front-line staff, they responded with slogans and catchphrases. It was difficult to get any sense of what their real thoughts or feelings were. It was painful to see honest, competent managers struggling so much.

After many months of preparation and uncertainty, the restructuring went through. Many local lead partners moved on – some to other firms, a few to senior roles in the new structure; others went back to full-time work as lawyers. Many capable junior staff 'jumped ship', leaving to go to other law firms. Administrative roles were filled largely by people who had been there before. A number of partners expressed disappointment that the restructuring had not resulted in more fresh blood joining the firm.

As the restructuring went through, the reported results continued to be satisfactory. When there was a problem the basis of counting was quietly adjusted and, 'hey presto', the numbers reported were good enough. Overall, the business climate was positive and the firm continued to record growth in income and profits.

At the end of it all Simon himself became increasingly disillusioned. He complained about the long delays in reaching decisions. He felt he had been blown off course by the prevarications of the senior partner. He had not been supported properly. It would have been better to grasp the nettle and show most of the local leaders the door. Privately, Simon took much of 'the blame' on himself. He felt it was his job to secure the necessary change and this had proved difficult. He was disappointed by many of the appointments to the new structure. It proved difficult to find the higher-calibre leaders that he sought.

After a number of years Simon left the firm and accepted an attractive offer to head a new American firm entering the UK.

As to the local practice leaders, they felt abandoned and unappreciated. They saw a vandal. For them 'change' was now a dirty word. Simon, they thought, did not appreciate all they had achieved. What he saw as a positive message of hope they experienced as an attack on all they had built over the years, and on their sense of competence. They felt let down by the senior partner whom they had trusted. They were bitterly disappointed that their earlier success had not been recognized. In their view the work of building successful local firms, the proudest achievements of their careers, had been needlessly 'thrown away'.

How do we make sense of this story?

Simon was a leader of change not so unlike many other leaders. He saw it as his task to 'drive change'. He was a missionary for new ways of working and he was not sure how long he would last in his leadership position. We guessed that evangelism and job insecurity both played a part in his motivation.

Simon had a clear story that he told himself. He felt that he had adversaries – those who needed to change but would likely obstruct his efforts to bring about the change needed. These were the local leads. He saw them as self-serving and hypocritical.

They talked loyalty to the firm and the importance of high standards as lawyers. Yet, in his mind, they were intent on defending their special interests which were at odds with the long-term interests of clients and of the firm. Simon felt it was his job to 'sort them out'.

In other words, Simon split the world into a version of 'goodies' and 'baddies' – those supporting the change he wanted and those resisting it. This was enormously satisfying. He knew quickly who was on his side and who against him. He could quickly make sense of all the complexities and uncertainties he faced. He could navigate a difficult situation, knowing what he had to do.

Having configured the task in this way, Simon could not really do business with the local leads. He was happy to 'engage' with them, talk and listen, but only on his terms. Either they agreed that the future lay with a united 'One Firm' approach, or the discussion would lead nowhere.

Simon also lived out a ritual that is widespread in current organizations. He got in a consulting firm to confirm what he had diagnosed but lacked the courage to say. He wanted an objective 'expert report' to justify what he set out to do. Without knowing it, he delegated the authority needed to be convincing as a change leader, someone worth attaching to personally and deserving of loyalty from below and above. In the eyes of the others, hiding behind a consultant's report is often perceived as defensive. Simon was experienced as an observer rather than an authority figure, able to relate eye to eye and to work together for a joint and better future.

Simon focused on staying close to those at the top of the firm. He developed ideas with them and he gained powerful allies. In the light of his experience of the client complaint, and challenges from other partners in previous leadership roles, he believed that managing upwards was the best way to stay safe.

Another interesting point for us is how much Simon took on himself. He believed that it was up to him to develop the vision, the way forward. It was up to him to persuade others to adopt the vision. It was for him to push through the change, with determination and patience, until it was fully achieved.

We also noticed the contradictions in how Simon handled himself. Very open and direct at some moments, at others he gave the sense of 'keeping his cards close to his chest'. The price he paid was that some saw him as manipulative. The contrast between the open Simon and the secret one led to disappointment, anger and resentment that destroyed the chances of the local leads becoming Simon's allies.

Simon bought into the dominant idea that it is all up to the leader; he trapped himself into believing that all that matters is the task and that his safety lay in being perceived at the top of the organization as a man who got things done. He was not in touch with the unintended consequence of such behaviour – those below feeling devalued, ignored and dehumanized.

Simon reckoned without the strong sense of community in the firm, both as a whole and in its many different sections, both local and regional; he reckoned without professional and other loyalties, and senses of identity. He ignored the history of the firm. He did not appreciate the web of largely unseen connections and loyalties that sustained the firm. He did not tap in to the community's desire for change; nor recognize its highly differentiated nature.

Simon believed that the vision of 'One Firm' would trump all these ties. 'One Firm' was potentially a powerful rallying cry. Many people were sympathetic to it. However, there wasn't a clear shared understanding of what it meant. Its value got lost because of the disappointment, anger and resentment caused by Simon's sweeping reorganization.

Indeed, we suggest that perfect abstract ideas – like 'One Firm' – do not help in situations like Simon's. They make it worse. We say more about this in Chapter 7 on communities.

Simon led change with a comprehensive restructuring. He commissioned a review by external consultants about better working processes, but what emerged from the review was a reorganization. The potential to develop a shared ambition of how the firm could work better in future was lost as partners and staff looked to their own futures. 'Will I have a job in the new structure?' they asked. 'Will it be something I want to do?' The change scenario turned into a survival drama.

In the end Simon invited what he feared. He provoked the 'us and them' feelings on both sides that he had anticipated. There was strong 'resistance' which frustrated the ends that he held dear. Simon was confirmed in his own mind as the solitary hero battling for change. And eventually he moved on to take up the cudgels in another organization.

What was it that drove Simon on? We can't be sure. We can speculate that perhaps it was early experiences, in his family or at work. We don't know. What we can say is that it was very powerful drive that had enormous positive value in terms of his energy, commitment and persistence – and also a negative side, in the expectation that Simon seemed to have, that he would have to be up in front, on his own.

What could Simon have done?

In our minds it started in Simon's head. Instead of writing off all the local leads as negative, he could have got to know them better as individuals, asking 'Who could I work with?' 'Who might I have common ground with?' 'Who has perspectives, experience, connections that could be useful?'

Had Simon seen himself as part of the social fabric of the organization he had taken over to lead, he could have tried to 'trade with' the local leads much earlier, before he was pushed do to do so by the senior partner. If Simon had taken the risk to be much more overt about what he wanted to achieve – about his passion for client relevance and for greater efficiency – he might have been a much more effective leader. Provided he enquired about others' ambitions and values, he might also have surprised himself with the amount of common ground between himself and staff, including those he pictured as adversaries.

If Simon could have had a more realistic, more human time-table, he might have been able to go faster in the long run. He would have needed to respect the experience of staff members and ask them for help in order to find a reflective and developmental way of making the change – meeting by meeting, as it were, not just in one go.

The social fabric

Organizations are much more than their formal parts – the organization charts, strategies and operating procedures. There is all the social fabric – the culture, ethos, relationships, trust, informal ways of working, shared values, understanding and beliefs, trust, corporate memory – that makes organizations live, just as consciousness makes us human. Anyone who has worked in organizations knows how important this social fabric is. It contains priceless assets that can make an organization special; but it is largely hidden, unknown and unappreciated. It is the social fabric that holds organizations together and gives them their shape and colour. It would be transformative if organizations viewed their social fabric as their social capital, and invested in them with due diligence, as they would with their technological and financial assets.

To quote Jesse Norman:

'*Edmund Burke argued that society has an order which links people together in an enormous and ever-shifting web of institutions, customs, traditions, habits and expectations built up by innumerable interactions over many years . . . Social institutions are ultimately grounded in feeling and emotion, which guide and direct man's reason. They are bound together by affection, identity and interest. They matter for three reasons. First, they constrain each other, competing and co-operating as required to survive, diffusing power across communities, and providing a social challenge to state power. Secondly, they give shape and meaning to people's lives, as work or play, setting rhythms to the day or year, creating overlapping identities and personal loyalties . . . Finally, institutions trap and store knowledge. Composed of myriad private interactions, traditions and practices as it is, the social order becomes a repository of shared knowledge and inherited wisdom.*

'The social order is not then the result of any overall design. It is not the outcome of any specific plan or project. It evolves slowly over time. Different social orders may evolve in different ways, and some may be more effective and successful than others. Each is sui generis, a largely incidental and historically contingent human achievement. It therefore makes an enormous difference how exactly each has evolved, and how it functions. Any practical or theoretical reflection on such a human artefact – and this applies to any institution, large or small, peoples and nations as much as words and ideas – must therefore begin with history and experience. How did it first arise, how did it evolve, and according to what principles, was its evolution continuous or in stages, was it fast or slow? What were its effects and what did it actually mean to those involved? For Burke, nothing human can be adequately understood without answering these or similar questions. All inquiry into human affairs, and all practical deliberation and action, thus begin with history.

'For Burke the social order is . . . sublime: it far outstrips human understanding.'

In other words, the social order in the shape of the network of relationships between people tends to resist being treated as a machine that can be re-engineered at will. No social encounter in your organization is free of the invisible hand of history and culture. Nor are the exchanges between you and anyone else free of the intuitive knowledge of how to behave, how to feel, how to think, how to compete and co-operate, and what to expect from each other. Each encounter is both free and, comfortably and uncomfortably, preshaped by what has already been learnt.

Assumptions underpinning our addiction to change

It is worth perhaps reflecting on some of the assumptions that underpin the orthodoxy.

We live in a period of unprecedented change

We notice that we have been here before. It is not the first time in human history that people have believed that they live in a period of unprecedented change. Heraclitus (who gave us the famous quote about change being the only constant) was an ancient Greek who lived in the fifth century BCE. Millenarians in the seventeenth century believed that conditions had reached the point where Christ was about to return to earth. William Wordsworth famously wrote during the French Revolution that 'Bliss was it in that dawn to be alive, / But to be young was very heaven . . .'

In the twentieth century, people from different perspectives have repeatedly argued that everything has changed. In the 1930s, for communists and fascists alike, global capitalism and liberal democracy were spent forces. The world was racing to a new future.

In the 1960s many felt a new age of social and economic liberation had dawned. In 1990, with the collapse of Communism, there was the so-called 'end of history'.

This time, there is a strange muddle. At the local level, in particular organizations and fields, we are asked to believe that everything must change; however, at the global level (Donald Trump's protectionism notwithstanding), the key structures – the

64

free market, liberal democracy, globalization – are said to have reached an end point and little need change.

We suggest that the absence of a proper historical sense is profoundly dangerous. Organizations that have no sense of history do not know where they come from or who they are. It means people have no perspective and are prey to every passing management fad.

Change is good for you

We notice that ignoring the past, disdaining the present and fleeing into an imagined perfect future is what totalitarian regimes have done, from Stalin onwards.

There was a young man who came to live in Moscow in 1935 (when Stalin's communist regime had achieved absolute control). He looked for a map in order to help him get around the city. He was told there were two maps that you could find. One showed how Moscow had been in 1914, before the First World War. The other was a picture of how Moscow would be in 1945, once the socialist utopia was achieved. The man had to navigate around Moscow using these two maps, one of the city long gone, and the other of an idealized fanciful future that would never happen.

The gap between reality and the ideal vision is perhaps typical of organizations and societies dedicated to being blindly rational, efficient and plannable. Such organizations also tend to live for the future and denigrate the present as part of a bad past. Change becomes compulsory in the service of a better future and is no longer seen as evolutionary; as a mechanism of adaptation to deal with altered circumstances.

We suggest that leaders also need to focus on continuity. Change and continuity are two sides of the same coin. You can't have one without the other. Individuals and organizations need change in order to sustain their essence. They need to be clear about what this essence is. And they need continuity for sanity and safety.

We notice that change is not always good. Constant upheaval can damage and destroy the social fabric that holds organizations together and makes them special.

We are interested in why the calls for 'change' are so prevalent in society now. Why do so many people – leaders and others – attach to change in the abstract? What is it about people and the current age that causes people never to be satisfied, always to look for more – to be addicted to change?

We suggest that leaders need to trust themselves more, to be kinder to themselves and accept the world more as it is. They would then come to a more realistic view of what change is needed and what continuity.

We also suggest that leaders need to see themselves as part of the change (and continuity) process. They need to model the change (and continuity) they want to see; to find out what's needed as they develop their own behaviours and values. It's the example people follow, not all the PowerPoint presentations and speeches.

People naturally resist change

We notice that 'change', in the abstract, has been reified and made into an object. We also notice that leaders are often keen on recommending change for others. It is less clear what change they are taking on themselves.

We suggest that the business schools and consultancies rejoin the rest of human culture. Change is not a thing that stands alone in life. It is part and parcel of everything we do. From the moment we leave our mother's womb we are all familiar with profound changes. We experience the whole range of responses, from joy to deep sorrow or denial.

We also wonder why leaders want to paint 'them' as hostile to change and 'us' or 'me' as able to lead change. What is it about themselves that causes some individuals to split people in this way? Many leaders seem to project their feelings of inadequacy onto others and the world at large.

We suggest that leaders need to trust their people. They should reach out and ask others: 'What change and what continuity do you want?' 'What matters most to you?' 'What is your vision?'

The role of leaders is to drive change

We notice the lack of results – leaders expected to drive change, yet the change that follows is constantly disappointing.

The picture of the lone hero at the centre of the stage, coming up with the strategy and forcing change, is seductive; particularly to the highly driven, personally insecure individuals who reach the top in many companies. But at what cost – to organizations and those in authority?

We notice the crazy burden that leaders are expected to bear. Magical transformations require magical leaders. Often leaders are expected to wave a magic wand and solve social and organizational issues that have developed over many years. No wonder so many leaders go from 'Hero' to 'Zero' in public estimation.

We notice the gap in perspective and experience between 'Tops', 'Middles' and 'Bottoms' in organizations. When we talk to board members, they often have the best of intentions. Yet what seem like rational sensible measures, when discussed in the boardroom, are often experienced by Middles and Bottoms as maddening, oppressive and abusive. Do Tops consider enough what the impact all their 'good ideas' will have when implemented far away in the engine rooms of organizations?

We have seen the failures when well-intentioned leaders talk about the need for 'change' in the abstract, and it is heard by many as an attack on what they do and who they are.

Organizations are not machines. They are living entities with dynamics of their own. Cause and effect are complex and unpredictable. It's not like driving a car – if you press here or turn there, you can't be sure which way an organization will go.

We suggest that a more doable, less fanciful idea of leadership is needed; one that takes account of the interdependence of leaders and those around them. One that acknowledges that many of the factors that lead to success are the properties of collectives, not individuals, and of the cultural and institutional infrastructure on which organizations depend.

We notice an increasing interest in the business literature in fostering 'collaborative', 'system' or 'distributed' leadership – people leading at many levels and in many places. What will it take to create the conditions for this wider leadership?

Questions to ask yourself are:

- Can you think of adapting to changing circumstances rather than wholesale, top-down restructuring?

- How can you involve the people closest to you?

- Which individuals and communities are you reaching out to, inside and outside your organization, to discover exactly what the problem/opportunity/issue is?

- How do others see the issues? What are their needs/perspectives? How do you encourage people to openly express their feelings about the problem/opportunity/issue?

- Can you use the need to adapt as a way to strengthen your authority and develop the people and culture of your team or organization?

In Chapter 4 we consider the third pillar of the current orthodoxy – how leaders are expected to come up with the strategy for their organization; what this means; the impossible burden it places on leaders, and what the alternative is.

CHAPTER 4

Strategy – Separating Reality from Fantasy

Strategy is the third pillar of the current orthodoxy (alongside heroic leadership and a preoccupation with change). If the job of leaders is to drive through fundamental change, then strategy provides the route map, the clear definition of 'Where do we need to get to?' and 'How are we going to get there?' In the orthodox view we often hear mention of 'gap analysis', comparing where we are now with where we need to be. Strategy is the vehicle for analysing that gap and coming up with clear thinking about what we need to do to fill it.

Strategy has come to hold an almost extraordinary mystique in organizational life. People with responsibility for strategy (and strategy consultants) get paid more than others, and are treated with a mixture of reverence, fear (and sometimes contempt) by those who work with them. Yet all too often we experience strategy as a document that sits on the shelf and has little impact on what the organization actually does.

We'd like to demystify strategy, and put it in its place. If you are leading (at any level in organizations); if you agree that organizations are living entities, with a will of their own; if you want to make a difference; what can you do? How can you use strategy productively?

First, a story.

The Honda motorcycle story

Here's an obscure quiz question for you. Back in 1960, which was the foreign country that sold most motorcycles into the USA? Was it Germany, the UK, Italy or Japan? The answer in fact was the UK. Wonderful big machines like the Norton Villiers and Triumph. By 1970, which was the country that sold most bikes in the USA? Yes, Japan. The Brits had lost out and the Japanese had come to dominate the US market.

How did the Japanese do it? Well, in 1975 the UK government decided to find out. They commissioned a report from one of the then emerging strategy consulting firms, Boston Consulting Group (BCG). BCG studied the situation and produced a report. They concluded: 'The basic philosophy of the Japanese manufacturers is that high volumes per model provide the potential for high productivity as a result of using capital intensive and highly automated techniques. Their marketing strategies are therefore directed towards these high-volume models, hence the careful attention we have observed them giving to growth and market share.' BCG said that the Honda strategy had been to start with small bikes, invest in production and marketing, learn how to dominate these markets and then gradually move on over the years into the markets for medium-sized and eventually large bikes.

It was a brilliant piece of analysis that became a classic, widely taught in business schools around the world. BCG became identified with the 'Experience Curve', the systematic reduction in costs that happens as cumulative volumes of production and sales increase. It was the key to the Japanese success, they said. Honda targeted the sale of small motorcycles to middle-class consumers. It sold the bikes in unprecedented volumes and thereby reduced its costs to world-beating levels.

In the 1980s, Richard Pascale, co-author of The Art of Japanese Management, *became interested in the story and wondered what he would find if he interviewed the managers who had achieved the success in America. He went to Japan and talked to managers in Honda who had been involved. They told a very different story from the BCG report. They talked about how tough it was to go to California in the 1960s and try to sell Honda bikes. Just 15 years after the end of the Second World War, they had a lot of prejudice to contend with. They were not allowed by the Japanese government to take much foreign exchange out of Japan.*

What was their strategy? The managers said: 'In truth we had no strategy other than seeing if we could sell something in the USA.' Their target was to sell the medium-sized 250cc and 350cc machines because these were the bestsellers in Japan.

What was Mr Honda's idea of how to succeed in America? Well Mr Honda felt confident because the shape of the handle-bars on the Honda machines looked like the eyebrow of the Buddha. This, he felt, was a strong selling point. (Bear in mind that the market for motorcycles at this time was black leather-jacketed types. No mass market existed for motorcycles in the USA as everyday transport.)

One year after arriving in the USA, a few of the medium-sized bikes began to sell. Then, as the managers put it, 'disaster struck'. The Honda machines began to break down. They acquired a reputation for unreliability. It turned out that the bikes were being driven longer and faster than in Japan and that they could not take the strain. Prospects for penetration of the US market looked bleak.

How to respond to the setback? As the managers said: 'events took a surprising turn'. In the first year Honda had not tried to sell the little 50cc Super Cub machines. They seemed wholly unsuitable for the USA where everything was bigger and more luxurious than in Japan . . . 'We had our sights set on the import market and the Europeans like the Americans emphasized bigger machines. However we used the Honda 50s ourselves to ride around Los Angeles on errands. They attracted a lot of attention. One day we had a call from the buyer at Sears [the huge US retailer] who was interested in buying the 50cc machines. But we hesitated to push the 50cc bikes for fear that it would harm our image in the heavily macho motorcycle market. When the larger bikes started breaking down, we had no choice. We agreed to sell the 50cc bikes.'

The rest is history. Sales of the little bikes took off. A whole new type of market was created as middle-class Americans began to ride on Hondas, first the little Super Cub and later medium-sized bikes. The new market was captured in the famous slogan 'You meet the nicest people on a Honda.'

How do we make sense of the story? What was the role of strategy in the Japanese success?

Strategy was mainly noticeable by its absence. It was the dog that didn't bark. It only emerged after the event, as a way for outsiders to make sense of what had been achieved. Honda's initial, loose idea of 'strategy' – attacking the existing import market with medium-sized bikes – did not work. The Japanese had an intention, an ambition to succeed in the United States, but the way in which they succeeded was something that emerged over time, as a result of trial and error. Strategy was the effort by outsiders – after the event – to make sense of what happened; it was produced by consultants to capture the Japanese 'magic' and bottle it so that they could sell it to other firms.

The 'dirty little secret' of strategy is that it is only clear with hindsight, and of limited value to managers in the moment, trying to work out what to do. The conventional idea of strategy is that you work out where you want to go and how you will get there. The glaring hole is the heroic assumption that you can think your way to success; that somehow clever people can work out the strategy needed in advance; that analysis and brainpower can substitute for being willing to engage with reality; that abstract thinking can replace experimentation, trial and error and the process of learning that happens as you try to put your ideas into practice.

It is often suggested that strategy is about 'seeing the bigger picture'. Well yes, it is that, and it requires us to try to apply our concept to the real world. Strategy, we suggest, is not about living with your head in the clouds. It requires the capacity to move from big ideas to engaging with reality, trying things out and learning from your experiments. It is about separating reality from fantasy. In the Honda story the modest and specific request from a customer to sell Honda 50s was responded to – because they, the managers believed they had no choice, it was the only survival option.

We suggest that the separation in conventional thinking between *developing* and *implementing* strategy is profoundly unhelpful. It says that the developing part is the clever bit; the doing or 'delivery' is mechanical and for lesser mortals. In fact, developing and implementing are intertwined; they occur together as people try to make things happen and as events unfold.

Honda did not spend any time bringing together teams of brilliant people in Tokyo to analyse the existing US market. If it had it might have learnt a lot perhaps about the existing products, markets, technologies and customers. However, it would not have learnt to create a new market and industry. Instead, Honda had a go. Its managers learnt by living in California and confronting the reality of trying to sell motorbikes to Americans. Along the way they had to let go of some cherished ideas about their products and about American consumers.

It is also striking that the key opportunity (to sell small bikes to Sears) arose from their day-to-day work and not any 'strategic initiative'. The Honda managers were just *being themselves* by riding their 50s bikes.

What marked the Japanese out was the way they responded to setbacks. The Honda managers were determined and pragmatic. They didn't give up, nor did they persist with an approach that wasn't working. They were able to use their eyes and ears and learn from the determination of their major customers to buy a different type of bike. We would argue that what differentiates successful organizations is not having setbacks, but how they respond. Are they alive to the potential of the situation and can they seize the moment? Can they let go of their own ideas, their own fantasies, and adopt other views of the situation (in this case a customer's) while retaining confidence in their experience and exercising their judgement?

Success in business and organizations does not come from having the right strategy in advance; it comes from having an idea or ambition and then sufficient variation and experimentation to learn in new situations. You can't shortcut the learning. You can't wish your way to success; you have to go through the difficulties. In this sense we agree with the old saying that 'Effective strategies are 10 per cent inspiration and 90 per cent perspiration.' Leaders going into an uncertain new area rarely end up where they expected. And as work proceeds, even their objectives change.

The dominant paradigm assumes that you can think your way to success, that the differentiator between successful enterprises and those less successful is the quality of thinking of those at the top. However, consider the great success stories of our time – Apple, Google, Vodafone, Facebook, the best healthcare organizations. What made the difference? Was it a clear strategy at the start? No! Lots of people have attempted, after the event, to rationalize what those companies and organizations sought to do. At the time, it was much less clear. It varied, of course – on the organization and the context. Courage, determination, shared ambition, expertise, ownership of scarce resources, speed of action, luck – they all can play a part.

There was a postscript to the Honda story. The controversy over the BCG report rumbled on for many years. Michael Goold, one of the authors of the BCG report, while defending it, agreed that: 'The report did not dwell on how the Honda strategy evolved. The perspective required was managerial ("What should we do now?") not historical ("How did this situation arise?"). The purpose of the report was "to discern what lay behind and accounted for Honda's success , in a way that would help others to think through what strategies would be likely to work."'

And there's the rub – separating 'how the situation arose' from the focus on 'what to do now'. As Burke would point out, without some sense of history we cannot understand where we are now, or what we should do.

Is the Honda story typical? We suggest it is. When you want to create something novel, when you want to go where no one has exactly gone before, then you are in the exciting and alarming position of having to create your own road map as you go.

And we suggest that the realm of the novel – working with a context that is significantly different from what you or others have encountered before – is much larger than the conventional view of organizations allows.

Strategies that sit on the shelf

We remember one of the Big Four international accounting firms that, with great fanfare, formulated a new strategy and then sent it to all the firm's partners around the world as a glossy document, assuming that they would implement the new plan – only for it to sit on the shelves of their offices, gathering literal and metaphorical dust.

People who have worked any time in organizations are familiar with the problem – that often there does not seem to be much connection between the formal strategy or vision of the organization and what it actually does. The strategy *sits on the shelf* while the priorities the organization actually has are different.

For the people at the top it is often a matter of acute frustration: 'The strategy is clear; why don't staff implement it? Why don't they execute better. Why can't they get on with delivery of what has been promised?' There is much talk about the difficulty of 'managing change', a suspicion that the 'resistors to change' are not being properly confronted, and a call for more 'leadership' at middle and lower levels to make change happen.

For people in the front line the issues seem different. The new vision, strategy, mission or plan often seems remote from the realities of daily life in the organization. They are not sure what is really expected of them. Corporate strategy can seem like an elaborate political game played by those at higher levels, jostling for power and position. Consciously or not, people in the front line often keep their heads down, thinking, 'It'll pass'.

For people in the middle the tensions are acute. They are usually preoccupied with the day-to-day issues of keeping operations running. They are weary of the stream of strategies and initiatives launched by would-be transformational leaders above them. If they are experienced managers, they are used to contradictory instructions from on high. That's not unusual. What's more difficult is when they feel torn apart by their sense of integrity and commitment to the organization on the one hand, and impossible demands on the other.

They don't know where to turn or whom to speak with honestly about the situation they face.

Heroic assumptions underlying the conventional way of doing strategy

- Nothing significant is changing while the strategy process is underway and nothing changes while strategic questions are being asked.

- The organization's world can be described adequately in numbers (and charts).

- People outside the organization will know better.

- Creating strategy is separate from implementing it.

76

- Failures in implanting strategy are the fault of the organization's people (the consultant perspective) or the fault of the strategy (the people's perspective).

- The future is predictable and controllable.

- The future can be extrapolated from the present.

- People are predominantly rational and reasonable, and are grateful to have the work done for them.

- People work for rational incentives (primarily) and not for each other.

- An organization's boundaries are easy to draw.

- Collaboration is straightforward.

- Events can be controlled.

How bonkers is that?

Strategy in action

As organization consultants and coaches we find ourselves less interested in the paperwork, the eventual description of what's been agreed and what people are trying to achieve, than in what's actually happening on the ground. Of course, what you're interested in depends on your view of organizations; conventional strategy work makes perfect sense if you see your organization as a machine-like creation, operating with high predictability in a generally stable context and amenable to changing its direction – like a car, being retooled and serviced so it can make different products, faster. This is the view of strategy that separates the plan (what's an appealing destination, how do we get there and how much fuel will we need?) from the implementation (actually travelling from A to B).

But most leaders don't experience their organizations quite like this. A less conventional, but perhaps more realistic and practical view, sees strategy as the pattern of priorities that an organization is actually working to (what Henry Mintzberg calls 'strategy in action'). These priorities emerge from the social interactions between people, which end up with a particular pattern so that the organization has a recognizable membership, purpose, boundary, culture, formal structure and outputs. Getting these things to be different is trickier than merely issuing a new set of instructions! As the old saying has it, 'culture eats strategy for breakfast'.

Putting strategy in its place

The problem with the conventional picture of strategy is not just that strategy does not lead to organizational success. Frequently, strategy is damaging to an organization's health, even its sanity. How so?

Strategy places an impossible burden on those in authority to anticipate the future and work out what will be needed. It ignores all the uncertainties of life and development. How can one person or small group (however capable) foresee the future and what will be needed? That's bonkers!

A focus on strategy traps those with authority into thinking that they have to come up with all the answers. It suggests to them that if they don't have a complete vision and strategy they are inadequate. Most leaders in our experience have strong ambitions and ideas – but a complete picture of the strategy – no! Thank goodness, we say. But the expectation of the top leader(s) to know, to have the magic wand, isolates them and makes it very hard for them to overcome the 'shame' of admitting that they need help.

In our experience it is essential to involve 'significant others' in working out where we are now, where we want to go and what needs to happen. Focusing on key relationships and bringing together the formal and informal organization connects the distinct parts of the organization. It joins up analytical and abstract knowledge and principles with the reservoir of experience in an organization. Last but not least, reaching out to others brings together strategizing and implementing in one process; and it makes sense to people because they are involved from the beginning and can begin to see the benefits and losses of strategic choices.

The top-down view of strategy is part of the heroic orthodoxy. It seems to us a fantasy, or fairy tale; a nice story to tell the children to help them go to sleep at night, but not bearing much resemblance to how successful businesses and organizations actually develop and adapt to altered circumstances.

Senior managers, business schools and management consultancies have done a great job of propagating the myth that strategy is for the few. In our darker moments, the authors have all spent time as 'strategy consultants' and managers. It is very seductive to be regarded by colleagues and clients as a tribe apart, and for it to be suggested that you have superior intellect and insight; to be ushered up to the top floor of powerful institutions, admire the splendid surroundings and sit down with powerful people to consider the future of their organizations. The taste and trappings of power and privilege can be intoxicating.

What we notice from our coaching is the toll the fairy-tale picture takes on leaders; the crippling mismatch between fantasy and reality – the sense of 'What I ought to do' being too far removed from 'What I can do'. The trap is for those at the top, above all. They can feel they are living a lie, pretending they know the answers. Such pretence can be corrosive.

There is a wonderful passage in the book War and Peace *when its author, Leo Tolstoy (who had been a soldier and knew something about the realities of military life), describes the actions of the*

Russian general Prince Bagration in the battles leading up to Austerlitz. At first you think, as a reader, that Tolstoy is mocking the general who rushes around in the smoke and confusion and seems to have no clear idea of what is happening, much less a master plan as to what his troops should do. Gradually you discover that Tolstoy admires the general. Everywhere he goes he encourages the men to do what they judge to be sensible in their local situation. He holds things together and gives courage to the men. In the chaos, it is all he can do – and it is enough.

Strategy is also damaging because it infantilizes 'the others'. It supports the myth that most people only have a role as spectators or extras hired to 'execute' the grand visions and plans. The majority of people don't feel seen, respected and valued by the 'parental' figures at the top of the organization, and so are invited to behave in the ways those at the top fear – to be childlike and inward-looking.

The trap is that people think coming up with a good and clear idea changes the world. If only it was that simple! One housing association chairman told us, in a moment of candour, that 'When a strategy or policy is written down, I think it is done.' It is a mentality we often encounter with politicians and civil servants. The document or statement becomes the reality. Actually getting things done and achieving results becomes secondary.

This separation of thinking from doing represents a particular and tricky challenge to governments, politicians and civil servants who work mainly through statements of policy (or strategy).

A focus on strategy can be damaging because it encourages wishful thinking; the grand plans, disconnected from reality, can endanger (or even destroy) organizations and their complex, sensitive and adaptive network of formal and informal relationships. Better to muddle through and trust in the living evolutionary quality of the relationship networks – which are all rooted in the division of labour and the real work with customers and clients – than come up with the strategy that is wrong, self-destructive or downright bonkers.

One of us worked as a young manager for the UK's General Electric Company, then run by Sir Arnold Weinstock. He remembers at the time longing for Weinstock to invest more and exploit the potential of the extraordinary technologies the company possessed. Weinstock did not want to do so and went on managing cautiously, extracting profit and building up a legendary cash pile.

Twenty years later Weinstock at last retired and was replaced by George Simpson, a man with a grand plan. He sold the defence and heavy electrical engineering businesses, bought a stack of telecoms companies in the United States and declared that in future the company – now to be called Marconi – would be a high-growth technology business. In two years the company was transformed – only it was not the transformation that Simpson had in mind. Far from being a high-growth area, the telecoms market crashed, acquisitions in America turned out to be hugely overpriced and the famous cash pile evaporated. Shareholder value of £35 billion was turned into half a billlion in just two years, and innumerable individual lives were turned upside down.

The curse of intellect

The tendency to mistake ideas for reality is pronounced among those who love ideas and numbers. It can become a curse for the highly intelligent – the bigger the brain, sometimes, the bigger the risk. For people who live in a world of ideas and are visionary, it is tempting to believe that you must be able to think your way to success. Implementation can be boring and disillusioning because it destroys the perfect alignment between the wished for and the real.

Focusing on being strategic

If the grand idea of strategy as the all-seeing, all-dancing plan from above is unreal (and sometimes downright bonkers), how else should we think of strategy?

Strategy means many different things to different people. (For more on different interpretations and what might be useful to you, read the classic work *Strategy Safari* by Henry Mintzberg and colleagues.) We suggest that the definition depends on you and the situation you are in; what makes sense to you and what will be useful in your context.

Our experience with effective leaders is that what matters is not so much the formal output, the strategy document, but how people work together on strategic questions. The verb, to be strategic, is much more important than the noun, strategy. Can we be and work strategically? Do we have a good enough sense of the landscape that we operate in, who the key actors are and what forces they are working with? Do we see how the world is changing and what we need to respond to? Do we have an idea of what our purpose is, what the reason for being of our organization is, and what part we play in that? Do we have a sense that we do have some influence, that there are things we can do now that will give us a better chance in the future? Can we relate what we need to do, here and now, to the 'big picture'?

In our experience, Henry Mintzberg is correct – successful strategies are discovered, not designed. And you have to work strategically in order the discover them.

Working strategically is what the people in Honda did. They did not rely on consultants or strategic analysis to decide what to do. They adapted and learnt as they acted. Critical was their judgement and use of intuition; something that is often hidden from view in descriptions of business success, the rationalizations, after the event. Honda managers did not rely on data gathering, analysis and rational debate. They made choices about where to go and what to do based on their experience. They could not explain fully after the event why and how they decided to do what they did; together they had some kind of collective wisdom.

We argue that managers and professionals of all kinds often know more than they give themselves credit for. They select questions to focus on and options to consider without knowing exactly why they do so. These judgements precede and underpin the rational data gathering and analysis that is often considered when discussing strategy.

Jeanette Winterson, author of such bestselling books as *Oranges Are Not the Only Fruit*, has remarked:

'There is still a popular fantasy, long since disproved by both psychoanalysis and science, and never believed by any poet or mystic, that it is possible to have a thought without a feeling. It isn't.

'When we are objective we are subjective too. When we are neutral we are involved. When we say "I think" we don't leave our emotions outside the door. To tell someone not to be emotional is to tell them to be dead.'

Winterson puts her finger on an important cultural pattern in modern society. Decision makers are expected to reach conclusions only when they can be 'sure enough' to know the probable outcomes and can insure themselves against risky exposure. Uncertainty is 'thought out of the system' and intuitive knowledge and emotional meaning are banned from the legitimate list of how to make sense of life, markets and organizations.

Handing on the baton – ensuring proper, delegated authority

A corrosive effect of the conventional, top-down view of strategy is that it leaves little room for those outside the boardroom to contribute their judgement and commitment to working strategically. Too often, in modern organizations, middle and junior managers experience micro-management. They are told: 'Just deliver!' It seems as if all their experience, their enthusiasm and expertise counts for nothing. When the weight of top-down initiatives, tick-box madness and measurement mania falls on them they wonder what they have to contribute.

One notable process for ensuring that organizations tap in to the commitment and professionalism of people at all levels is the 'Mission Command' approach now used in all NATO armies and which originated with the Prussian/German Army in the 1860s and afterwards (see Stephen Bungay's book, *The Art of Action*). This deals with the age-old question of how to ensure coherence in a huge organization while responding to changing circumstances and allowing professionals at all levels to input their expertise. It allows all staff to work out what they are required to do (exactly) and then negotiate what they will contribute.

The process addresses the issue: What do you do when the unexpected occurs? The originators of the process were more honest than many business people about the amount of uncertainty and chaos there is when you try and implement your strategy – as the Prussian general, Helmuth von Moltke, famously said: 'No plan long survives contact with the enemy.' They also recognized that generals often interfere with operations and give orders without knowing the local situation, sometimes with catastrophic results. They came up with the approach of 'Directed Opportunism', in which senior officers make really clear what is expected of different units, and why; they limit direction to defining and communicating the intent.

A key principle for senior officers is: 'Do not command more than is necessary, or plan beyond the circumstances you can foresee.' At each level, more junior officers are given freedom to adjust their actions in line with the intent. They are expected to use their knowledge of local circumstances, and their initiative and independent judgement to decide how to achieve the objectives set. A careful process of 'Back Briefing', of negotiating objectives and the necessary means, links the different levels of the hierarchy. Far from asking for mindless obedience to orders, the modern military seeks people at all levels who can think for themselves and act accordingly.

Why is this important? Because so many companies and organizations do not ensure proper delegated authority. We meet many senior, middle and junior managers who wonder if they are respected by those at the top. What scope do they have to use their expertise and initiative? As they understand the local circumstances, why are they not able to act on what they know? Why can't top management make clear – really make clear – what the intention is and then let them, at their level, get on with it? Why is there so little trust?

And the process, of course, works both ways. If we want to be trusted by our bosses, we also need to trust those more junior in the hierarchy. We need processes for 'staying in touch' while recognizing that we are all often not in control. We need to think through how we develop judgement about the capacity of others. Who can we trust? To what extent? How do we develop trust in others? What experiments are needed? And when do we need to get out of the way and let others get on with it?

'Best Research for Best Health'

We compared notes at the morning coffee break. More than 100 senior researchers, managers, funders, regulators and others had come together in Church House in central London to consider the future of health research. We had a quick 'huddle' with members of the new R&D director's team who had each been sitting on different groups for the first session. The mood was one of relief and excitement. 'They like it!' said one of the team. Before the meeting there had been a lot of anxiety about how participants would respond to the new direction proposed by the director. Now we were hearing that people not only liked it, they also identified with the underlying purpose of the proposed changes.

The new director of R&D had been in place for less than a year. Based on her lifetime of experience as a clinician and scientist, she was passionate about the different place that she wanted research to have in the health service. She wanted research to be not just a backroom activity but something available to all patients and carers, driving improvements in treatments and health across the NHS.

Over the course of the one-day meeting, the director discovered that her vision was shared by many others. There was potentially a powerful social cause to which many different individuals and groups would commit. Other meetings around the country followed.

The support of ministers and civil servants was critical. In a way that her predecessors never had, the new director took the initiative to approach the Cabinet Office and the Treasury. It turned out that the chancellor – then Gordon Brown – had a very personal interest in supporting health research because of his son's chronic illness. An unprecedented amount of money – £1 billion – was negotiated to support the new agenda. Another key ally was Simon Stevens, then the prime minister's special adviser on health and later chief executive of NHS England.

The ground for a new strategy was laid carefully over a number of years. Critical was face-to-face mobilization of a network of senior researchers and clinicians and negotiation with key players by the new director. One of the great capacities of the new director was an ability to be very forthright. She was well known for grasping nettles and saying exactly what she thought, but she could also be very sympathetic and skilled in forming strong personal working relationships.

The new strategy for research broke new ground in bringing together the themes of health and wealth. It was clear from the outset that the Treasury was interested in providing major new funding if there would be an economic gain from the new approach. The Treasury was excited by the potential of clinical research in England being a world-beating activity and a major generator of wealth. For many of the director's colleagues in the NHS, this was a matter of suspicion. They felt they should be working for the good of the public, not profits for commercial companies. However, the director was determined to reach out to industry – both the big pharmaceutical companies and other smaller, high-growth companies. She was determined to find the 'win–win' in dealing with these outside groups

After more than a year of preparation and negotiation, the document 'Best Research for Best Health' was put together. Given that the director needed support from across government (and was bidding for large sums of public money), it was essential to have a formal strategy. The document was signed off by the health secretary, Cabinet Office, Number 10 and the Treasury.

A new organization, the National Institute for Health Research (NIHR), was established to take responsibility for the strategy. It was established as a virtual organization, able to adapt quickly to changing circumstances and keep a place at the top table in the Department of Health and the rest of Whitehall. At the head of the NIHR were the director and her deputy, who worked as a double act, focusing on the areas in which they excelled – she the relationships and vision, the deputy on translating intentions into the documents and agreements needed across government and with other research funders.

The director and her deputy were insistent that each major part of the strategy be accompanied by public, web-based 'implementation plans' that were dated and revised every six months. The intention was that the overall strategy should be a continuing 'work in progress'. It would be improved and developed as circumstances changed and as the R&D team learnt more about how to achieve their objectives.

The new strategy was not welcomed by everybody. Part of the plan was that money would be withdrawn from hospitals across England and reallocated on the basis of open competition, in processes overseen by international experts. There were winners and losers. At the time many people around research and development (R&D) thought this was too big a change for the system to accept. The vested interests would be too powerful and would stop money being taken out of major institutions. There were major battles, for example when one northern city did not win the funding they believed they should. There were even strong protests from a few local MPs. In the end the decision of the international panel was only upheld when ministers in Whitehall backed the R&D director, explaining that they could not subvert the process of open, public competition.

Ten years on, the NIHR has become an accepted feature of the health landscape and been praised by health researchers around the world.

The story of 'Best Research for Best Health' illustrates a number of themes we described in Chapter 2. The new director of R&D built a 'working majority' for the radical changes in research that she wanted to make.

She was unusual in the web of relationships that she had developed across health and health research. Throughout her career she had sought out difference, for example spending time on a secondment with the pharmaceutical giant GSK. She came across as very direct, but also someone with strong values and who could be very sympathetic and supportive at a personal level. When she shifted into a leadership role she expanded her network. She involved 'more than the usual suspects'; she engaged with patient groups and she built up links abroad. The director targeted individuals and communities. She sought out those in positions of authority, including many whom her predecessor had not thought to involve. There was a boldness and directness about the way she approached people.

All these links were the critical resource that she could draw on once she had landed the top job in R&D and set out to lead radical changes. In leading, cohesion comes before coherence.

If you want different results you need different conversations. If these conversations work well, then action flows quite clearly and naturally. You don't have to force it. However, we're not under any illusions about the difficulty of this for leaders and strategists. These conversations take time to set up and conduct. While good analysis and clear, rational thinking is still needed, these conversations require leaders to cope with disagreement, confusion, politics, resistance and criticism. It's more uncomfortable than issuing a glossy document telling people what the plan is, but in our view much more likely to get people behind you.

The director shifted the nature of conversations that happened within and across R&D. The Church House meeting was one of a number in which different stakeholders came together and looked openly at the current situation – the barriers – and what should be done to improve matters. For many participants the meeting felt fresh and invigorating; there was an honesty to the proceedings and a sense of hope that they had not experienced before. Tough issues, such as the sometimes problematic relationship between universities and the NHS, were talked about openly. The new approach advocated by the director gave people hope that translational and applied research would have a new priority.

At her best, this director embodied the combination of being forthright and being able to listen. She listened carefully and tuned in to the needs and desires of others, while stating her own views very plainly. People came out of meetings and conversations with her emboldened to act on their convictions. They had been involved in serious conversations and they had enough fun to want to go on and get engaged.

'Best Research for Best Health' also demonstrates how timing is all-important. The first conversation we had with the director about developing a new strategy for R&D was in 1998, seven years before she landed the top job as director of R&D at the Department of Health. She had sought advice on how to develop a strategy and what to include in it. At that point we agreed it would not help to seek to develop a new strategy for R&D – the critical ingredients for the process of development and change that she sought were not in place. There wasn't a shared under-standing of what the problem was, much less what the potential solutions were. The necessary allies had not been assembled, and not least, our client at that stage was a regional director of R&D and did not have the positional authority to lead a big change.

In 2005, after our client became national director of R&D, the position was very different. Now our client could assemble the team that she wanted; she now had the credibility to go to senior people in government and beyond to seek their support. Putting the essence of the changes she wanted into a document was essen-tial if she was to gain the support she needed from ministers, civil servants and others.

A key feature of the approach used in the NIHR were the evolving 'implementation strategies' that supported the new approach. Implicitly, the director recognized that context matters. No one had been down this road before. Therefore trial and error and careful experimentation were essential. In a more candid moment the deputy director acknowledged that 'NIHR is all one big experiment'. This was not something he could say publicly in Whitehall where it can be difficult to admit to mistakes. However, it was something he could say and act on privately. The implementation strategies were therefore updated over time as circumstances changed and as the leaders learnt from experience.

It was not always easy, but the leaders showed that they could tolerate confusion, uncertainty and disagreement; that they could hold their nerve about being in charge but not in control. They were willing to act when others were overwhelmed by the appar-ent uncertainty and chaos.

Questions to ask yourself:

• What do outsiders need to see in terms of strategy so that you look professional and competent?

• When is it necessary and helpful to work on formal strategy?

- As a new leader, can you claim space and time to listen and enquire/scope first?

- Do you have to be seen to be formulating the strategy yourself or can you share responsibility with key others?

- Who do you need in the room to avoid a split between development and implementation?

- Can you take responsibility for strategic adaptation with your people and avoid them feeling alienated, infantilized and helpless?

- How do you look after yourself and avoid taking on mission impossible – for the sake of the health of the organization and yourself?

- What's working well, what not so well, and what needs to change?

- What's special about your organization and how can you sustain it?

- What seeds of the new are there in the present?

The heroic orthodoxy

As we have explored in the last three chapters, the current orthodoxy in organizations has three elements:

- Transformational leadership, in which extraordinary individuals have the vision, charisma and resolve to see what is needed and make others follow them. The 'vision' is then implemented or 'delivered' by managers who bring order and predictability to the world. Plans and targets, metrics and audits, checklists and protocols ensure that people do what is intended.

- A relentless focus on (and addiction to) change which matters above all else in these times of ever-faster economic and social development. The job of leaders is to drive through the change needed.

- Strategy that provides the route map for change. Strategy can only be undertaken by a few at the top who have the intellect, vision and ambition to see what is needed.

The three elements make up an 'unholy trinity'; they are all aspects of the same set of beliefs and assumptions. The common thread, as we discussed in Chapter 1, is the need for leaders to drive through change.

With regard to each element of the heroic orthodoxy, there is a wide gap between intention and impact. Managerialism has supplanted leadership, the addiction to change efforts mask and contribute to organizational inertia, and strategy becomes a political game, remote from the realities of serving customers and users. Unintended consequences rule.

In the last 40 years this cocktail of beliefs and practices has become dominant as the business and political worlds concluded that change towards markets, competition and choice is imperative.

We suggest that the heroic orthodoxy does not work, indeed is frequently counter-productive. It relies on magical thinking, and is divorced from reality 'on the ground'. It has many unintended consequences. It eats away the social fabric on which organizations depend for their success; and it discourages individuals, at all levels, from leading in the way organizations need. The implicit message is: 'Keep your head down; do as you are told; don't think for yourself; don't take the initiative!' An orthodoxy that espouses strong individual leadership in fact sabotages the distributed leadership that organizations need. How bonkers is that?

So how can you lead your organization and adapt to changing circumstances? If organizations and communities are living things, what can individuals do to foster healthy development – how can they keep the organization sane? If the heroic orthodoxy, with its emphasis on individuals driving change, is damaging, what are the alternatives?

We now lay out a different approach, exploring what successful leaders do to make a difference.

Instead of taking the whole burden on their own shoulders and feeling a need to do change *to others*, they reach out and are focused on building alliances across groups and organizations.

Instead of appearing to try and change it all, they show they are respectful of what they inherit and curious to find out how and why things have evolved as they have.

Instead of appearing to denigrate what people have done and who they are, they appreciate what has been successful *and* take a hard look at what is not working.

Instead of being missionaries for 'change' in the abstract, they identify specific issues that need to be addressed and that they hope will resonate with others. They explore whether there is enough common ground for action.

Instead of telling others what is needed, they frame questions that invite others to contribute.

Instead of seeing 'culture' as an immovable object that stops them achieving what is needed, they recognize that culture is alive and all around them, 'the way we do things around here', which is continually adapting and shifting as circumstances change. They play a part in influencing this development.

Instead of pushing 'change' into the future, they take responsibility and work here and now to make a difference.

Finally, and fundamentally, they take their own experience seriously. They learn to live well with the anxiety of not knowing how things will transpire while offering a lead. They appreciate that the future is created and shaped by being part of something, with others, and so they learn to rely on the group.

In Part 2 we lay out our response to the heroic orthodoxy, beginning by exploring what it means to take our own experience seriously in order to become the settled (enough) self. In a book that emphasizes the collective nature of leading, it may seem strange to start with the individual. However, that is the resource that each of us has. We can't take responsibility for the world. We can and need to take responsibility for how we respond to it – by becoming the leader we can be (and not the one we think we ought to be).

PART 2

Becoming the Leader You Can Be

CHAPTER 5

The Settled (Enough) Self

We start our exploration of the alternatives to the heroic orthodoxy by considering your relationship with yourself. How comfortable with yourself do you need to be to lead in organizations today? How confident? What role does self-doubt (which is so common) play?

The idea of the self has been examined by philosophers, psychologists and social thinkers for a very long time. What we notice in organizations today is how essential it is to take some time to settle yourself enough, and not to get caught up in abstract ideas of heroic leadership – or remorseless self-criticism. Our experience is that it is not simply a question of confidence or self-belief; it is more subtle and interesting than that. You need to have some sense of who you are and what contribution you make. And, at the same time, leading is unsettling for the leader and the led – taking risks, making a difference, means upsetting existing power relationships and familiar ways of working together. It offers rewards and comes at a price which is not knowable in advance.

We suggest that in order to lead we move around on the settled–unsettled continuum.

Being unsettled gives us energy and purpose, and we are motivated to take the initiative. Leadership happens in the moment. I am unsettled by what's happening; do I step in and say something? What? Do I keep quiet and let the moment pass?

We know leading when we see it because we experience significant connection to another person that is more than what we

The settled–unsettled continuum

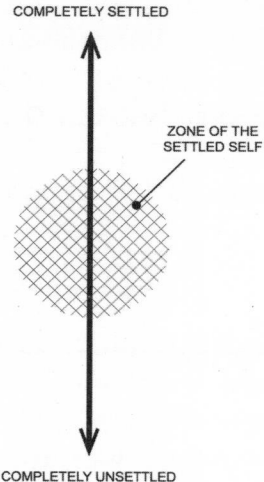

COMPLETELY SETTLED

ZONE OF THE
SETTLED SELF

COMPLETELY UNSETTLED

think about the situation. We become a part of something that is more than rational. We see someone who is offering us the opportunity to join them in being a part of something not yet defined. There is relief that someone has spoken out, stepped in or stepped up in a stressful situation. There is hope that from now on things might be different. We will follow them. As followers, we might experience their speaking out as courageous while the leader experiences an internal compulsion to act. They are unsettled, troubled and touched by the situation in some way and can do no other. It is likely (probable even) that in the moment they do not have a well worked out plan or strategy, and reflecting on these critical risk-taking moments leaders often say that 'I couldn't have done anything else, I couldn't let it go, I had to say something'. They were compelled to act in order to be themselves.

Being yourself and a part of something

The philosopher Paul Tillich asserts two inseparable aspects of the courage to be: 'The courage to be is essentially always the courage to be as a part and the courage to be oneself, in interdependence'.

98

Leading means being *you* and being *a part* of something simultaneously and inseparably. This can be enlivening and affirming, and it can tear us apart; we know that if we hold ourselves completely apart from others we are not leading and we fear that we may lose our identity if we become too absorbed in the group.

Being yourself – being a part continuum

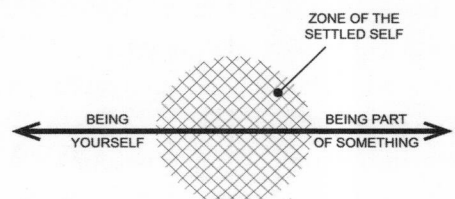

Just as we cannot know day without knowing night, we cannot know what it means to be settled without knowing what it means to be unsettled. Similarly, we can only be ourselves with and through others. A leader must learn to live with these twin polarities – being yourself and being apart, being settled and unsettled.

Settling yourself *enough*

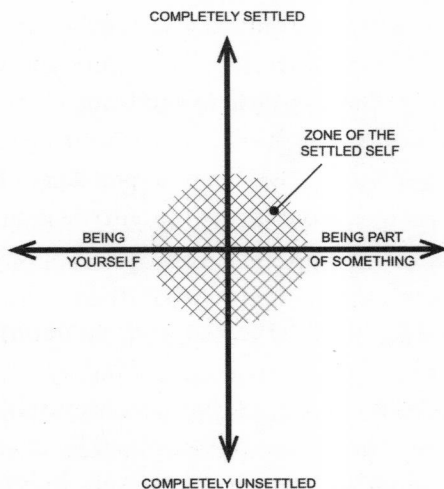

They develop over time the capacity to be comfortable in themselves, in the presence of others.

Leaders frequently find themselves both at odds with and dedicated to their organization and their colleagues at the same time, unsettled and yet still a part of something. They respect what their organization stands for and what it has achieved, but aspects of how it is and what it does frustrate them. This is the crucible of leadership practice – what will you settle for? Without the courage or the commitment to act, you are part of the problem. If you become too frustrated and unsettled you can only leave or pretend to be something you are not.

To focus on the individual (which much of the leadership literature does) is always limited and partial. We never lead alone. Even in those quiet moments of reflection we hold in mind what others think, say and do about the situation. Furthermore, while there is only one you, you occupy different roles – parent, child, boss, subordinate, leader, follower, expert, novice – depending on the different situations in which you participate. So you settle and unsettle yourself within and between multiple situations, because experiences in one situation that you are part of will affect and inform what it means to be yourself in a different situation that you are also part of.

The leadership tightrope

There are acute, enlivening moments when we are *being ourselves* and *being a part* of something in an uncomfortable situation. The leader and the group feel anxious. The anxiety may be expressed as energy, excitement and enthusiasm, and it will be tinged with fear and doubt. Leading can be like walking a tightrope, and we need to be able to keep our balance in conditions of high anxiety. It is to be expected that we will fall off the tightrope sometimes, so we need some safety measures in place so that (even though we may be hurt) it will not be fatal, and we might learn something about ourselves and our organization. The safety net is, as it were, the relationships we have and the groups we belong to. We think it is critical that leaders are conscious of these *settled–unsettled*, *being yourself and a part* dynamics and find ways to work well with them. It is in these moments that we shape the story we tell ourselves about ourselves and our leadership. Here are a couple of stories that demonstrate how this works.

The first concerns an executive team of a multi-million pound organization on retreat; things are getting tense.

'Show no weakness'

Mike, the chief operating officer (COO), is struggling to be understood by the rest of the team, and patience is wearing thin. After a while one of us intervenes with the comment, 'I think Mike is trying to say "I am carrying too much responsibility for this organization and it cannot continue."' The director who was most exasperated with Mike is astonished. 'I thought you were saying the opposite and that you wanted some of my staff to report to you too; you were trying to take over.' A short while later the CEO asks Mike 'Why couldn't you say for yourself that you are carrying too much and it is not sustainable?' After a pregnant silence he says, 'Because if I said that you would think I was weak.'

How your story shapes your leadership

Mike had convinced himself that, above all else, as a leader he had to be strong. To admit any weakness was to admit failure. This meant knowing what to do in every circumstance and 'leaving feelings out of it'. The executive team that he worked in would, typically, call a halt to proceedings or move on to safer territory if emotions were running high. In the relatively recent past they had experienced a bullying and vindictive board member, and it had been unsafe to say 'I don't know' because they would pick on you. Even without this history, teams are often reluctant to speak plainly to each other about what they feel as well as what they think. We 'don't want to upset anyone' or we fear we will fall out and fall apart so 'keep our feelings out of it'; but in so doing we create a perfect trap for ourselves.

For Mike's team his admission of weakness broke the established pattern of relating. Something previously unspeakable had been spoken. Saying it out loud created an opening, a crack, a possibility that the group might have a new conversation if they chose to pick it up.

The choices that we make in these moments are critical. If the conversation does not develop, if there is an embarrassed silence while the group look at the floor, then Mike and the group end up in a worse situation because they have all been shamed in some way. Mike had done his best to create the impression that he did not need anything from the team. He was well liked and highly regarded, and since he had taken up the post, performance had improved significantly. The last thing that anybody wanted was to lose Mike. Unnoticed by his colleagues, he was paying a high and unsustainable price for this. The team, unspoken and unintended (and with Mike's full co-operation), had created a situation that none of them wanted, and they most feared. Mike was not being himself; rather he had cultivated the role of invincible COO, keeping him and the team apart. He acted as if he had what some psychologists call a 'false self', designed to serve an idea of how he was supposed to be.

Mike thought he knew what a good COO was like. What became unsettling, intolerable even, for Mike was that his day-to-day experience of being COO was increasingly in conflict with what he was telling himself it *should* be like. He had internalized the orthodox story of what it is to lead. There was an ideal type of leader who could change the world by their own efforts and force of personality. It was everything he was not.

Here's a second story.

Be 'a *proper* leader'

Dan came to one of us for coaching because, he said, 'I need to be a leader and I'm not'. This was surprising. He was a highly educated professional man in mid-career. For the past three years he had been a director of a large technology-led change project. Five international organizations that were usually in competition had formed a consortium to purchase and run the same expert IT system across their organizations. As well as giving them much greater purchasing power, the common system allowed them to share scarce professional expertise.

Recently the new system had been implemented in Dan's own organization. It had not gone well. Things were getting sticky with the supplier and Dan was beginning to wonder whether they were up to the job. He used the system himself so shared the frustration of his colleagues, but felt he couldn't say that to them because he was a director of the consortium and felt responsible. To acknowledge it was not going well would risk failure. He has to lead and this means coming up with answers.

I ask Dan to talk about a time when things were going well and he tells me about how the five organizations came together. He was instrumental in this. He spoke to the CEOs and professional heads of each organization before he went to see the people who ran the service this new system would support. He knew that one of the first things they would say was 'I would like to work with you but my CEO won't wear it', which is why he made sure he had their permission. He knew from his own operational experience in his own organization that this service was struggling and he thought it was likely that all the organizations had similar problems. So, on his visits he asked about how things were working. He was amazed by what he found. There were common problems but also complementary problems in the sense that smaller organizations had different problems from larger organizations, and they could help each other. However, each saw the other as a competitive threat.

Dan took time to get to know the five service heads and then invited them to a meeting. 'All I did was ask them to tell each other what they had told me.' For the first time the service heads realized that many of their worst fears were unfounded. Competition was only a small part of the story. If they co-operated in procuring a common system they all stood to gain.

I suggest to Dan that this story told a lot about the kind of leader he was when he was at his best. How would he describe it? 'But that's not leading' he says to my amazement. 'So what is leading?' I ask and he goes on to describe in abstract terms how leaders are decisive, determined, visionary and persuasive. He was not this. All he had done was talk to people about what was going on and, magically, they had all signed up! He had muddled through and made it up as he went along. He could see what could be achieved if the five organizations could work together; he could see it was both a big 'if' and a massive prize. He was both excited and diminished by his excitement. 'Little me' would never be good enough to pull this off; he had to be transformed into a 'real leader'.

The effect of idealization

Idealization is central to the dominant heroic orthodoxy. As we have seen, strategy is for the few and requires us to create abstract pictures of an idealized future.

'Competency frameworks' for leadership and management roles are another example. The frameworks are an abstract expression of an ideal leader. It is something to aspire to, but we know (because we are human and imperfect) that we will fall short. The point is to *strive* for perfection.

The struggle between ideals and working out how to apply them in practice is, of course, age-old, going back at least to Plato and Socrates. Socrates was a difficult customer. He was not interested in idealization and abstraction, only with *how we should live now and how we can take responsibility together and individually*. This was to be discovered in conversation and debate, fully employing our critical faculties and questioning everything. Eventually this led to his death when he became too much for the city authorities. Nevertheless, he bequeathed to us the Socratic method of sitting in a circle as a social group, thinking together about issues that matter to us rather than following someone else's ideas, mindlessly as it were.

In Mike's and Dan's stories idealization is alive and well. For Mike, weakness is a sign of failure because, ideally, leaders must be strong and unemotional. Dan had swallowed Platonic ideas about the ideal form of a leader and he knew it wasn't him. For both of them, being fully themselves was something to be avoided. For Mike to be himself would mean acknowledging he was not super-human but had weakness like the rest of us. For Dan it would mean questioning the received, conventional wisdom about leadership. In both cases they believed that to make these acknowledgments would mean they were not leading. Both were attached to a vision of leadership which rested on an implicit denigration of themselves and the people who worked for them. Rather than working with the people as they are, they clung to the belief that they themselves and the people were inadequate and in need of reform.

The courage to be – the leader you can be

It is in the continuous interplay between being yourself and being a part that we discover what it means to be settled and unsettled. For Tillich, we cannot know what it is to be ourselves without knowing the anxiety of non-being or nothingness. The fear of nothingness can drive us into ourselves and to search for self-affirmation through endless reflection on our inner self. Alternatively, we set others up to give us approval or confirm our self-doubts. This anxiety is familiar to leaders who fear being found out (imposter syndrome), being rejected, insignificant or ineffective. Equally, because we fear not being a part of something, we may give ourselves up to the group or organization in an unquestioning acceptance and compliance, so that it becomes our identity and we are nothing without it. We become a slave of the rules, status and hierarchy and abdicate our co-responsibility for what happens.

As we have seen with organizations that have gone badly wrong (Enron, Lehman Brothers), senior people are susceptible to creating a separate, self-serving world for themselves, and in so doing, pervert the whole way of how things are done in their organizations.

Leadership theory that focuses on the individual is not only empty but damaging. If leaders see themselves as separate from the people they are leading they are not only kidding themselves, they are seeing themselves and others only as a means. Tillich writes: 'A self which has become a matter of calculation and management has ceased to be a self. It has become a thing'.

Blaming 'the system'

A modern version of this way or ordering the world is to refer to 'the system' as in the 'accounting and auditing system' or the 'political system'. The system becomes a thing; something fixed and separate. We are a consumer of the system or we are only an unthinking cog in the machine system. Yet, leadership (and for that matter, citizenship) is about making a mark, making a difference in some way and leaving traces that we were here.

For Tillich, it is the courage to participate *in spite of* this knowledge that transforms our anxiety into courage. We see the world for what it is; we don't fly from it into abstract and idealized fantasies. We see that despite our sophisticated systems, life does not run like clockwork. Buses run late, people get ill, the road floods, there is an accident on the motorway, someone dies unexpectedly, our phone call is not returned and the dog gets out of the garden. We doubt the people around us and we doubt ourselves. Who am I, little me, to take any initiative here? Yet in spite of this, never mind poverty, hunger and war, we find the courage to be ourselves *and* participate with others in order to change the world.

Choosing your story

Dan could have 'chosen' to tell himself a very different story about himself. He could have told himself that he was smart; that he was capable of reading organizational politics because he anticipated that the first (defensive) response of the service heads would be to hide behind their boss. That he was good at gaining the trust of his professional colleagues; that they valued the fact he was 'one of them' and listened to their concerns. He took their experience seriously. He could have told himself that he used this professional and personal credibility to bring the group together. That he was self-effacing and made it clear that he was not doing this for himself but for the good of the service. He could have told himself that by not making a PowerPoint presentation and claiming the big picture and insights for himself he allowed the group to find their own way and become part of something.

Instead Dan allowed himself to be captured by the tyranny of the business schools' definition of leadership, which was everything he was not. Dan also 'chose' to tell himself the expected version of what a leader should do because our brains are less self-contained than we think; even when we are thinking alone we are holding others' (on whom we depend for praise) feedback and

107

respect, in mind. In that sense we are making decisions in association with others, albeit subconsciously.

No absolutes

We know there is no absolute objective truth about a situation, and that means that the position or perspective of the observer is pivotal. So Dan's choice about the story he told himself was not a choice between right and wrong, because both stories (and other possible stories) have justification, or 'evidence' if you prefer. The story that is told rests on the position that the author chooses to take, in the presence of others, and for a leader this involves following the group enough but retaining an 'independent' position.

You cannot do it all, no really, you can't

Let's consider Sarah's story.

Sarah is a leading television producer. Over the past few years she has become more and more senior in her company. At first she was a reluctant institutional leader, and still struggles to accept bureaucracy. She thinks of herself as a leader in three areas – production, business development and management. All three matter and are interdependent. It is not just about her own projects but also about creating an environment in which colleagues and the company can grow. She has used her scepticism about bureaucracy to good effect. She makes careful judgements about which meetings she needs to attend to be effective and keeps this potentially time-consuming activity to a minimum. She recognizes that there are some risks in this strategy too because she might not be visible enough or seen as a 'team player' by senior people, 'not one of us'.

So far so good, but the strain is beginning to show. Reluctantly she has reduced her own business development to a minimum and now she is worried that her own projects are suffering. She has a backlog of creative ideas and several big projects coming to an end that she needs to replace. Recent proposals have been unsuccessful. She made the choice a few years ago to stay with her current firm and she retains that commitment. They have been successful in recruiting good staff from around the world, and now more people are relying on her. There is too much to do and she cannot do it all. The senior people that she grew up with have retired or left, and recently her primary mentor died. She feels alone with the responsibility and pulled apart.

Sarah's story illustrates the many choices that we have in relating our own story as well as the material differences that these choices make. Perhaps the most unsettling insight for a successful leader to accept is that, as you become more senior, you can't do it all; you have to choose. Of course we make choices all along, but often we are choosing to stop doing things that we don't enjoy or are not good at in favour of those we want. Sarah's career, and more fundamentally her identity, was built on seeing herself as a broadcaster and a leader; she wanted both. She would gladly have set aside the politics of the company but she recognized that it would be fatal to her leadership ambitions.

Sarah's response was to channel her energies into building bridges between business development and production. She had worked successfully in both areas and so embodied the value of working across what often seemed like separate, parallel worlds. Sarah worked with a colleague to create a network through which people could better connect to the mutual benefit of all. By being herself she was also able to become a part of something much bigger and offer others the opportunity to join her. Sarah's other response was more of a personal struggle, which was to see the world of administration differently. For years she had steered clear of that world and looked down upon 'administration' as a dirty word. It was for 'men in suits' who had lost their way, and now she was one of them. This too was unsettling.

Settling yourself enough to lead

We have arrived at an interesting point. We lead because we are unsettled about a situation in some way. By leading we further unsettle ourselves and those around us. The inertia of organizational life, and sometimes the willful acts of other people we unsettle, threaten to kill off our leadership. We discover that we have to make compromises and to accept that we (and the world) are imperfect. 'Muddling through' may be as good as it gets. All the time we have to contend with the siren voice – which maybe our own, a colleague's or the latest transformational consultant – telling us that real leaders are different (if only you could be more like them!). Real leaders do not doubt themselves; they are clear, certain, dedicated. We may also tell ourselves that leaders are born not made; that we missed out in the leadership lottery so are stuck. Perhaps the only way out is an MBA or that transformational leadership programme . . .

These beliefs and assumptions are so deeply embedded and pervasive that we swallow them often without realizing, and so we feel powerless.

We want to offer some alternative beliefs and assumptions that are grounded in the day-to-day experience of leadership and organizational life, and which are much more hopeful. Leadership is a craft that we learn from our own experience. We learn with others what it means to be a part of something, but nobody can learn what it is for yourself to be yourself. That's *your* job, and becoming an effective leader requires you to become a sufficiently settled self.

We can craft our leadership, but it requires practice, as Mike's story illustrates. As we have seen, Mike struggled to make himself understood by his team. Mike's 'don't show weakness' mantra was experienced by others as 'I don't need you', so they stepped back and allowed Mike to do all the work. He became frustrated with them for not taking up their responsibility, so became more and more directive.

Understanding your authority

The orthodox approach to developing our leadership (which many of us have swallowed, including Mike and Dan) is to focus on our weaknesses. This can be extremely damaging. The work that Mike needed to do for himself and with those around him was to enquire into the nature of his authority. What does he say and do that others experience as inviting and authoritative, so much so that they want to follow, not because they have been told to do so but because they want to be part of creating something with him.

If you understand the source of your authority then you are more likely to be able to say, even in a stressful and pressured situation, 'I don't know' or 'I can't think'. That is not an expression of weakness; it is a disclosure that at this point in time you are 'unsettled', and an appropriate expression of vulnerability. It is a recognition that you are not all-powerful or all-knowing, that you cannot lead without being unsettled and that you cannot be yourself without being part of something with someone else, which means that you need each other. It is an invitation which can be gladly accepted because others like to take part and gain recognition by making a contribution.

In our work we notice how hard it is for leaders to hear what their colleagues value them for. When we conduct a '360 (degree) feedback' we deliberately use appreciative questions and ask a neutral question about what an individual might do differently.

If we think about the arts, we expect to applaud artists for the way they practise their craft. We are intrigued if we are exposed to their studies for their most famous works. We don't interpret their repeated experimentation and practice as a sign of weakness. In football, we don't criticize a striker for being a poor defender; their authority in the team is as a striker. So my first job as a leader is to understand and practise (with and through others) what it means for me to be myself skilfully and authoritatively. Of course, I also need to pay attention to the ways in which I undermine myself and give away my authority, but that is not the place to start.

Pause to reflect and consider the context

Costs of not being settled enough

Before we focus on what you can do practically to settle yourself enough, let's look at the other side of the coin. What if we are not settled enough to lead effectively? What are the consequences? Here's a story to illustrate.

Ed was the COO of a large organization. He worked in tandem with the visionary CEO. Ed was the one who interpreted the bold statements of the CEO (they both joked that the CEO did not know what he meant until Ed had converted the CEO's statements into strategies and plans). Over the years they had negotiated a way of working together that made the most of their different styles and skills. The CEO was the public face of the organization, and people appreciated that Ed was critical to its success. They were a very effective double act.

Ed was good company, but increasingly took on a different persona. He had a powerful intellect and prided himself on being on top of all the issues. He was clear that only he and the CEO had the full picture; therefore only they could take the key decisions. Over the years his need for control became oppressive for people in his team and for those further down the hierarchy. His immediate team became ciphers who would not take the initiative or make a decision until they knew Ed's view. More independent-minded people refused to join the team, or if they did, soon left. Managers talked about being passed a 'baton on elastic'. They were asked to take responsibility, but as soon as an issue got 'hot' the baton was seized back. In meetings, middle managers would often say: 'I am not sure Ed would approve of that.' He was an invisible presence in many discussions.

Ed got through an enormous amount of work but still there were long delays. Even quite minor items had to wait for his approval. In the end Ed drove himself close to exhaustion in the months before he retired.

What struck us as outsiders about this story was the gap between Ed's intention and his impact. Ed said he wanted to provide a clear lead and to control only the big policy decisions. In other words, he wanted to be part of something – the team. In practice, middle managers seemed fearful of any decision or initiative. They felt they could not act because of fear of how Ed might react.

Losing it!

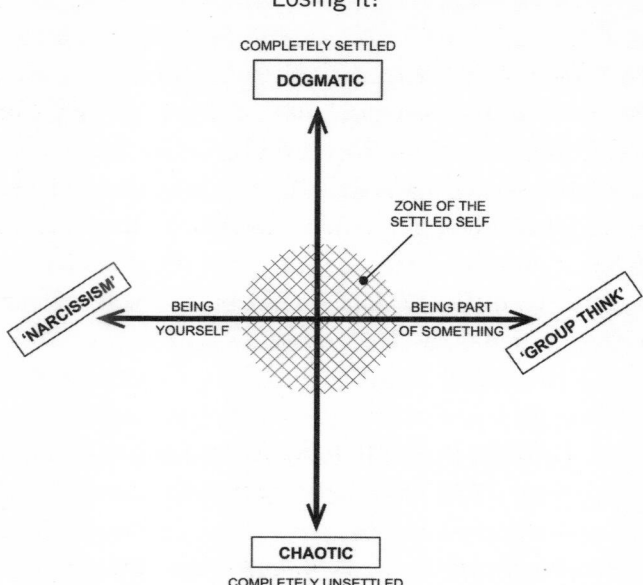

So, unintentionally, Ed found himself well out of the zone of 'settled enough self' and trapped in the Dogmatic/Narcissism corner.

It wasn't just about Ed. There was a long history in the company of top-down control. The impact of the charismatic CEO, always demanding more, was important. Yet Ed's own drive to succeed and control, his relentless need for more information, did seem a critical part of the picture. From the outside we could not know for sure what drove Ed's behaviour. We did know he had refused an offer of coaching, saying that there was too much personal stuff that he did not want to explore. Our sense was that Ed's relentless dissatisfaction with himself drove him on. He could not bear to see others handle things in a way he did not approve of. He could not bring himself to trust himself enough to trust others.

How to settle yourself enough to lead

Settling yourself enough is critical to leadership. It is not self-indulgent nor is it always enjoyable – it can be tough. Nor is it a once and forever event. Finding our balance, holding ourselves 'in the zone' of the settled enough self, requires you to pay exquisite attention to your own experience and that of those around you. This is what it means to practise the craft of leadership.

Here are three different aspects of settling yourself and what you can do to practise them.

1. Settle yourself by knowing your story and keeping it up to date

Nature and nurture play their part in making us who we are. From an early age our experiences of being included, excluded, listened to, ignored, successful, unsuccessful and so on shape the story we tell ourselves about ourselves. This story turns up in and shapes our habitual ways of responding, particularly when a seemingly new situation reminds us of previous experiences. We may feel we belong to a profession or group that is inferior in some way, or superior. We may feel that our education, gender or race entitles us, or disqualifies us. We know that in general terms these things have a real impact when we look at the prevailing pattern of who gets which job, for example.

When examining our own story we must think in particular, not general, terms. Just because something is generally the case does not mean that it is *your* case. Indeed, we can use these general patterns to free ourselves of responsibility. If only certain types of people are listened to around here and you're not one of them, then you need not feel irresponsible when you fail to speak up against something intolerable. You may have had previous experiences of being ignored, but how will you find out if it's true in these circumstances? So it is important to keep refreshing your views with your recent experience. For example, when you doubt yourself is that telling you something about what's going on now, or is it an old script of that you are rerunning?

The leadership literature is full of words that are hard to pin down; words such as 'authenticity', 'presence', 'gravitas' and 'authority'. We think that all these things have their root in being yourself; that is why it is so important to understand the story you are telling yourself. If we are not capable of being ourselves then we lose all authenticity, presence, gravitas and authority. At the heart of this process is the question 'What is the source of my authority as a leader?' Our authority does not exist in the abstract; it is both internal, what we know about ourselves (the story), and social. The internal story might not change very much but we are likely to find ourselves in many different situations and it is important for us to understand the nature of our authority in each and every situation. We discover this by noticing how others respond to our authority as we exercise it. Our position in an organizational hierarchy is part, but only a relatively small part, of our authority. We do not have to compete with others for authority. Our authority grows symbiotically with those around us, as we become ourselves and a part of something.

What you can do

Take your own experience seriously – it's harder than it sounds! We think it is important to have a place where you can work with your experience. This may be a professional coach or someone who has your interests at heart and is at a distance.

Keeping a diary or journal is a useful way of reflecting on your current experience. Writing helps us to make sense of the world. When we stop and look at what we have written we see the story that we are telling ourselves about our situation and ourselves.

Questions to consider:

- What kind of leader are you and how have you come to think of yourself in that way?

- Which experiences formed and inform your approach? How recent are they and what is the effect they have on you?

- When are you at your best, feeling confident and authoritative? In which situations do you feel much less powerful?

- What are the different stories behind these scenarios? What other, different stories could you tell about these situations today?

2. Settle yourself enough to show up, prepared but not complete

In his story Dan accepted the dominant orthodoxy that the purpose of preparation and personal reflection was to work out what you want, where you want to get to and how, so you can direct others. Everything needs to be thought through. In fact he was turning up *prepared but not complete*. He had prepared well through the contacts he had made and in thinking about what might be possible. He turned up to each and every encounter sufficiently confident not to need to know the answer to everything. He was able to explain why he was there; he could see potential advantage in working together. He was prepared but he stopped well short of seeking to persuade.

By asking questions he discovered their differences and that the situation was more complex than he had anticipated, and richer with possibility. Had he been 'complete' (certain and dogmatic) he would not have been alive to these possibilities.

This does mean being settled enough to articulate clearly what you mean, want and don't want. Not to impose your will and prove that you are right, but to free others to do the same; in doing so we take up our authority and responsibility. We are, in effect, issuing an invitation for others to join us and to shape the future with us.

What you can do

What do you feel most certain (right) about in your leadership at the moment? How do you know? Who thinks differently about this? Go and find them and stand in their shoes.

Think about a significant encounter that is coming up. How are you preparing for this encounter? Are you gathering an arsenal of arguments and weapons to make sure that you can win? Challenge yourself. What don't you know about this situation? What are you curious about? How might you put forward what matters to you and show up with some good questions?

Settle yourself enough before the next encounter

3. Settle on what you can do here and now

The leadership literature is full of heroic stories of bold moves, but for most of us it is not like that, most of the time. It is not about a single thing and giant steps, but making gradual progress on several, but not all, fronts. Sarah's story tells us that we cannot have it all. As the reach of our leadership increases so do the demands. Leaders often speak of 'spinning plates' and the need to keep them all turning. Bluntly, you can't; you have to choose to keep some going and to let others fall – or give the plate to someone else. If you choose to do the latter, then you accept that it is now *their* plate and they may allow it to fall.

To stretch the analogy further, having settled on the plates that matter to you, how fast do they need to spin and what does that require of you? We meet a lot of leaders who complain about what they cannot do because of what they haven't got. Usually what they haven't got is within another's gift and out of their control. Often there is a degree of fantasy involved too in imagining that with whatever they haven't got – for example, the support of the board, more money or staff – everything would fall into place and life would be straightforward. A better question to ask is 'What can I do with what I have, about the thing that is concerning me?' You may well discover that you already have enough of what you need to make a difference. Of course, this is a much more demanding position because you are required to take responsibility rather than feeling sorry for yourself.

What you can do

Consider a meeting you attend regularly. When does this become predictable, following the same unproductive pattern of conversation? Does this matter to you and are you unsettled by it? Be prepared, when you see this pattern occurring, to draw attention to it. You don't need to have a specific alternative in mind, simply to draw attention to the recurring pattern: 'This is what we seem to do every time and this is what it makes me think or feel.' Don't let the group off the hook too easily. Hold them to considering what is happening. Once everybody sees the pattern it is much harder for the group to carry on repeating it.

When you call to mind a situation that seems stuck or problematic, who is in this situation with you? When you talk to them about it, how does that conversation go, usually? What could you do to prompt a different conversation? This may mean saying something different – a question or statement – or it may mean doing something different – going for a cup of coffee or a walk.

Changing the conversation is a critical skill to practise. It comes from being settled enough to be able to detach from the issue itself, notice what's going on inside you and what's going on in the group. Then being prepared, in the moment, to put that experience in front of the group, requiring them to consider it.

If you can settle yourself enough then you can find your place and power with other people. You can lead and you can follow because you are part of something, with others. In the next chapter we examine the sometimes baffling ways in which groups operate, and how you can lead in, through, and with them.

CHAPTER 6

Finding Ourselves in Groups

There is a strange thing that happens in today's organizations. We know that we depend on groups for performance, yet we persist in focusing on individual conduct and behaviour. We 'talk team' but measure and reward individuals. We hold individuals accountable for the performance of groups and organizations. When it comes to leadership, attention is all on individuals, their competencies, qualities and skills, their behaviours and actions. The focus on the individual leader driving change is central to the current orthodoxy in organizations.

In this book we argue that performance, motivation and creativity are not so much a matter of single minds, but more a phenomenon of groups or a network of connected groups, in a social community and a specific historical moment. We suggest that leading happens *between* people; that it is the product not of one person's qualities and skills but a function of how people relate together in a particular situation. So we need to pay attention to the task (the work the group has to do) and to the relationships (how individuals and the group work together). We argue that it is essential to think about both task and relationships as a matter of routine. You can think of this as working both *on* the table and *off* the table. The task, expressed in the formal agenda, is *on* the table and the group dynamics are *off* the table, in the sense that they are usually unexplored. We often hear that groups are too busy to spend time on relationships. We say relationships are too important to ignore.

121

This failure to consider the dynamics of groups can have tragic consequences. A series of inquiries into scandals (we're thinking, for example, of the Challenger space shuttle disaster or car companies producing fraudulent emissions) has shown that people were well aware of the problems that led to disaster but that they were not discussable in groups and therefore never saw the light of day. When they do consider groups, senior managers often try to constrain what happens. When we are asked to facilitate a meeting, many clients say something like 'but nothing too touchy-feely' or 'pink and fluffy'. They will often go on to say something like: 'We want some clear, hard outcomes that will be implemented'. The clue is in the language, of course. The fear of intimacy and of feelings is denigrated by their being described in female terms, 'pink and fluffy', and contrasted sharply with male 'hard outcomes'.

In this way the leader and the team are trapped into having an unreal and abstract conversation that may produce some clear statements on a flipchart but which will not generate commitment to doing anything. In order to avoid disagreement and debate, groups act as if deaf and blind to the reality of their situations.

In this chapter we explore what it means to work well together – how to look reality in the face; how to discover genuine commitment; in other words, how we find ourselves in groups.

It's normal to be apprehensive of groups

Why are groups so neglected? How has this happened? Groups are often a bit scary; they cause us to be unsettled and uneasy in our own skin. We experience dynamics that are powerful, but we are wary of turning over too many stones for fear of what we might find. Although we depend on groups to get things done, we remain very ambivalent about being in a group; being just one of many. Group membership lends us a sense of belonging, recognition, position and identity, but we also have a sense of wariness towards groups as we know that they might take us over, bring the worst out of us or label us as 'deviant'. These tensions and anxieties are ubiquitous in all groups, even those that function well. The tension between being yourself and being a part of something is inescapable.

Professional groups such as doctors, lawyers, teachers, managers and engineers are very prone to this kind of ambivalence as they hold the ideal of vocational independence dear, viewing any attempt to control what they do as oppressive and misguided. For this reason many of them become leaders, despite their best intentions, because that way they feel they can retain their sense of autonomy and independence from group norms.

When we lead we often prefer to deal with issues one to one. That way, we believe, we will keep control and avoid being overwhelmed. Yet the group dynamics do not go away. They keep rearing up. This can be a problem, or if we are prepared to go there, a reservoir of potential.

We need to be conscious of how groups work at times of critical incidents; when things go well and not so well in situations of stress. To understand the Jekyll and Hyde nature of most group members we need to reflect on how each one of us learns how to be in a group, relate to authority figures and co-operate and compete with peers. Typically it is our critical experiences in the family, school, adolescent peer group and career that shape how we experience group membership.

If we are able to get in touch with the strong feelings that groups can stir in us (fear, delight, anxiety, joy, shame, anger, pride and more) and work with others to make sense of them, we can be much more powerful as leaders.

This willingness to explore what's happening in the work group is all the more important now that we live an in age of 'Permanent Transition'. It is as if the reality of the organization is socially and psychologically a building site and reconstructed on a daily basis. When organizational structures keep shifting and bosses move frequently, what and who can we attach to? We need something to hold on to in order to be able to work effectively. We need some sense of security and belonging if we are to keep our wits about us. Groups that function well can provide that sense of security and belonging.

Joining a group

When an individual joins a group something changes; something that is not fathomable by reason alone because the impact of joining and belonging is an emotional experience, rooted in our intuitive knowledge of social and collective processes. We wish to belong to a group and yet we fear it because of anxieties shared by us all – rejection, bullying, being made to feel small and incompetent, and being 'found out'. Perhaps for these reasons all cultures have evolved meeting rituals that have the unstated purpose of containing such anxieties and putting people in touch with their intuitive knowledge of the hidden rules of social interaction.

The English tend to avoid the danger of being dragged into a boundary-less conversation on entering a group by talking about the weather as a first point of contact. Kate Fox has called this a 'grooming ritual' in her book *Watching the English*. Talking about the weather gives people the chance to regulate distance and familiarity; and they can begin to guess whether to engage as equals or in a lower or higher status position. The weather talk also allows both parties to get an inner sense of how open this person is to engaging with you, whether you can get on and whether it will be easy to co-operate or there is conflict lurking beneath the surface. In other words, we have rituals of tuning in to each other, and that is why we recommend that leaders pay attention to 'settling in rituals' and to the 'context for co-operating' in a group.

The Scandinavians have evolved very helpful rituals of social bonding and potential reciprocity before the joint work in a group starts. Meetings often start with coffee and Danish pastries, and enough time is given to the process of arrival and checking each other out that everyone has met everyone else and feels safe and ready to start work in earnest. This may also include singing a folk song together. These rituals also deal with the disrupting effect of late arrivals and offer a space in which absent people can be contacted and reminded of the invitation to be part of something that is too good to miss.

Work in, through and for the group

Leading a group

Groups need leaders (not necessarily the person with formal authority), particularly in critical moments when the group gets stuck. What is really going on here? What do we need to focus on? What is doable and important? What are we neglecting? How are we working together? How might we improve? What's not being said? What do people want to commit to? Are we doing what is needed to meet our objectives? What is needed next? Any of these questions may need posing in the moment if the group is to be effective. You will notice that some of these questions relate to the task that the group is working on and some relate to how the group is working. A key skill of leadership is the ability to read the group and judge what needs attention *now*. This does not mean that the most senior member of the group has to take responsibility for all these things – some will do it more naturally than others. The job of the most senior person is to make sure that the group attends to these questions in some way.

In our research for our book *Living Leadership*, it became apparent that a great number of employees and leaders brought a deep need for reassurance about their sense of place and security in the current organization to each group meeting. Group members looked to the leader to take charge in a reassuring way, and wanted them to be 'first among equals'; to help the group move from one agenda item to the next and end the session in an authoritative way. They looked to the leader to communicate a sense of trust and belief in the group. In response to meeting these fundamental emotional, social and practical needs, the group reaffirmed their loyalty to their leader and legitimized their authority. Once a group had a sense of being one group (but not all equal) it was able to engage fully with the work – and the implication? Leaders need to pay attention to the social fabric of the group and ensure that it legitimizes their authority and develops a sense of secure attachment to them. People work for people, not abstract documents or perfectionist, fanciful targets.

Understanding the health of your work group

Many of the satisfying moments at work are connected with the experience of a group working well together and completing a challenging task in a joined-up way. Groups that function well produce more than the sum of individuals' input. Equally, many frustrating memories are associated with teams and groups failing to gel and live up to their potential. The decisive factor that stops a group performing is the network of relationships in the group malfunctioning in some way or another. We all know from personal experience that scoring points off each other and squabbling about territory gets in the way of co-operation. The conflicts, tensions and uncertainties of the wider organization are often replicated and replayed in the drama of the meeting.

The leader takes primary, but not exclusive, responsibility for paying close attention to how the group is working. They need to consider the amount of energy in the group and whether conversation is realistic and demanding. They need to notice individual contributions, who is speaking and who is not speaking; what is being said, or left unsaid – and the *pattern* of communication in the group, whether it is functional or dysfunctional. The key capacity is the willingness and ability to tap in to your own feelings: 'What do my emotions tell me about what is going on?'

A useful assumption for a leader or participant to make is that the person who disengages or expresses distress rarely does so alone, but expresses those feelings and anxieties on behalf of the group. It helps the group and the leader when they or another member notices what is going on and expresses what they notice. Naming what everyone can observe in this way removes the shame barrier and creates the opportunity to discuss openly what is making group members uncomfortable. Handling such a potentially difficult conversation honestly reassures the group and builds confidence that the group can do its work.

Paying attention to feelings is not a luxury or a diversion. The feelings are there for a reason. If we can face them and consider them, then we can be of service to the group. This work usually needs to be done *with* others. Until we talk out what's inside us we are not clear what we think and feel. Leaders need at least one trusted person with whom they can 'say it like it is', particularly in periods of uncertainty and transition. Having sought counsel in this private way, it is crucial that the leader has the courage to name the issues that make everyone anxious or hinder progress in the group. Otherwise the world is split into 'private safe', 'group unsafe', and this will spread distrust.

In our experience, the challenge is often greatest for those holding formal authority in the group. They can find it very uncomfortable, sometimes impossible, to get in touch with their feelings, which seem too unsettling and dangerous. That's when having trusted colleagues can make all the difference – people with whom you can express your thoughts and feelings openly, and who can help the group focus on what is needed. That is why you need to work on settling yourself enough to be able to work with your group(s).

Breaking the pattern of a group

Groups (often very quickly) fall into habitual ways of working in which everyone knows their role. This helps us to feel comfortable and at home in a particular group, but over time it can become dysfunctional and cause the group to feel stuck.

At this point it requires a courageous member of the group to intervene. Consider this story.

We were nearing the end of the two-day meeting of the international Information Technology group that we had been observing. The group met once every quarter. Sven, the Danish boss of the group, was summing up. He went round each member of the group, commenting on past work, giving out marks for performance and handing out assignments for the next three months. He was like a schoolteacher, handing out end-of-term reports. When he was only halfway through the group, Thomas, who was the other Dane in the group and who knew Sven well, interrupted him: 'Why do you treat us like this, Sven? We are senior professionals. Don't you think we have our own ideas about what our priorities should be? Why don't you ask us?'

You could have heard a pin drop. There was a period of silence. We wondered what would happen – whether Thomas would keep his job, whether Sven would be able to 'hear' the challenge.

It turned out that Sven could work with what had been said. He did not shout Thomas down nor move onto something else. He allowed the group to talk about what had emerged. There followed a passionate and generous conversation about the leadership of the group – what had worked in the past and what was needed now. The group was clear that it did not need a schoolmaster. What it wanted for the future was what they called 'an oil-can leader' – someone who could smooth the way and make the links between IT and the different operating companies. Sven had these skills and links. He was a natural diplomat. He knew the bosses of the different operating companies around the world. Professionally Sven was an accountant and so there was little value in him directing the IT professionals in terms of their understanding of the technology. On the other hand, he could be very valuable as a link to senior executives around the world.

The exchange we witnessed did not, of course, emerge from nothing. There was 18 months of history. Sven had (prior to the meeting) taken time to go and see each of the members of the team and talk with them. He himself felt supported by us as outside coaches. Thomas felt a strong link with Sven; partly because of shared nationality, partly because of a shared perspective about what the corporation needed.

We had helped the group say what it thought by facilitating several open review sessions. We had played back some of the themes we had heard in conversations during the breaks about getting real about the group's targets and resources.

In responding to Thomas's challenge, Sven for once stopped calculating what he ought to do and acted instinctively. He was troubled by the challenge and fearful of the emotions that might be released if he picked up the challenge. The stakes were highest for him; his own sense of competence and his reputation around the company. However, he was also determined to learn how the group could improve and develop. He felt supported enough to take a risk and explore the topic of his own way of leading, which up till then had been partly off-limits. It turned out to be a critical incident. After it the group could never go back to previous ways of working.

Responding well to the challenge was the making of Sven's leadership. The 'oil-can leader' turned out to be the way to bring together his talents and of operating with the group's needs.

Multiple loyalties and Cabinet responsibility

Sven, as is often the way with members of powerful teams, carried the team with him; held it in mind as he worked on the team's behalf. He felt responsible not only to himself but to team colleagues. He recognized and nurtured interdependence and showed appropriate loyalty to colleagues.

It is common for the woes of an organization to be blamed on the senior team. In difficult or uncertain times the senior team is often accused of being indecisive and not offering clear enough direction. How the individual members of the senior team respond when they hear this from other colleagues is critical. Often these will be informal 'water cooler' conversations, perhaps even light-hearted banter or gossip. This becomes a test of loyalty for the senior team member – how to respond? Colluding with the idea that a complex situation is simple and that the senior team needs to find magic solutions weakens the authority of the whole team. Speaking up for the team, on the other hand, sends a strong signal that the team as a whole can be relied upon.

Of course, it is in the nature of today's organizations that we often belong and feel loyalty to more than one team and this can be tricky. Sven was a member of the senior management team as well as the head of the IT team. Many still harbour the fantasy of 'alignment', as if it were possible for there to be no tension or conflict between the different groups and teams of which you are a member. We explore this further in the next chapter when we discuss organizational silos, but for now we need to note that being loyal to each team and holding appropriate boundaries between them is critical to leading groups effectively.

Gossip is a gold mine

Given the dominance of the heroic orthodoxy, it is often difficult to 'say it like it is' when speaking to bosses or people in competitive units. The real conversation is driven underground and dismissed as gossip. What can you do if you want to find out what is really happening and how people are feeling? People have different solutions. Some invite others to the pub; some people go for tea and cake. You can't ban gossip! But you can hear and make sense of it and then explore ways to bring it 'back in the room', so that you can make progress as a group.

Consider this story about the cabinet secretary and the heads of administration in a regional government in central Europe.

We were asked by the minister of state (in the UK it would be the cabinet secretary) to 'abolish gossip' (his words). The official purpose for the work was to bring about a change in working practice so that people would 'talk to each other in meetings – and not about each other in the canteen'.

Unfortunately, this was a long-standing client so we couldn't act on our instinctive desire to walk away from such an absurd request. Absurd because gossip is the force in a tribe or group that holds the network of social relationships together. It does so because it remains informal and free from legal regulation and political control.

Knowing this, we set about designing a workshop. We invited the officials and leaders of the government to present to each other what they were working on, what they needed from each other, and what they thought about the way that they worked with them and the people under them. We gave ourselves the role of 'basketball coach', with the right to call 'time out' at critical moments in the workshop/meeting. This allowed the group, its leader and the consultant to reflect together on the relational aspects of the meeting.

The purpose behind this process was to make conflict possible within the group without people feeling too threatened. The fear of conflict and of honest conversations is present in many groups and organizations. Given the hierarchical nature of society, leaders of organizations are always scared of the group ganging up on them. Equally, the group is always scared of being bullied or over-burdened by the leader. If we could take the presence of this fear more seriously, rather than denying its presence and power, there'd be a lot more energy in groups available for creativity, passion and basic effectiveness in getting things done.

The fear of open conversation is what lies behind much of what appears to be 'bonkers' in formal group conversations and meetings. It is also the reason why people need to gossip in places like the canteen and the toilet. People need spaces in which they can be honest with each other and get some relief from the anxiety that builds up as a result of controls, pretence and double-talk.

Back to the workshop. During the breaks we visited the subgroups and split them into smaller private groups, to conduct a short brainstorm after each break. We asked them to collect helpful ideas and practical hints gathered via the informal organization and its gossip. These findings were then posted around the room for all to read. In addition, each half-day, before the real work started, small break-out groups were asked to say good things about the people they had gossiped about and share any helpful ideas for their joint work. These ideas were also posted around the room.

After lunch on the second day a member of the group asked to say something before we started: 'It's been obvious to me that the real intellectual work has been done in the breaks and in the gossip sessions. Therefore, our purpose should not be to stop gossiping, but to stop organizing meetings the way we do. They are so formal that no one ever reveals what they really think and could contribute!'

This comment liberated the group and a discussion ensued about what actually happened in meetings. The key insight that emerged was that leaders needed to pay attention to energy flows in the room and leave a space on the agenda for people to discuss what they normally gossiped about, before or after meetings. It also became clear that it was unreasonable always to rely on the leader to notice everything going on in a meeting. All members of the group were asked to say what they noticed, what they knew, and what they felt needed to be explored. In this way the collective commitment to decisions could be strengthened.

Over the years that followed, this 'impossible' workshop had a significant impact on the senior management team, where the decisions of the various ministries were co-ordinated. Group members were able to find the courage to confront the dominant leader of the group – while the group leader learnt that he could afford to trust people more. By consciously suspending his distrust, he discovered that the heads of the various ministries were capable of working to an appropriate standard and with political nous. Instead of complaining privately, the boss challenged the bureaucrats to take more account of political realities.

Consequently, the awareness grew that the work of the government got done through the interdependence of two aspects of organizational life – the formal and the informal. Step by step, bridges were built between the two. The group became more discriminating in understanding the different contexts that fitted different types of communication and working things out with more subtlety. It was agreed that it was perfectly legitimate to want to control communication with the outside world, but this was counter-productive when overused in informal internal networks.

Harrison Owen developed his 'Open Space' methodology because he noticed that the most valuable conversations at conferences were in the breaks. It is a useful source of ideas.

Coffee conversation – Join up the formal and informal organizations

Exploiting differences in the group

Through the process of bringing gossip and informal conversation into the room differences were exposed and could be worked with. We encounter potential leaders who are reluctant to say what they think, and others who are preoccupied with being right. Neither is useful if we are trying to be part of something and create a team. Charles Handy uses an unpleasant, inaccurate but nonetheless powerful analogy of the frog that doesn't notice the gradual increase in the temperature of the water until it is too late. Leadership groups that cannot hold their differences end up in 'group-think' because they have developed a shared and fixed view of the world. So as leaders we need to be capable of taking a step back from the group (even while we are in it) to spot what is going on.

It's when there are conflicting ideas, interests or perspectives in play that problems become stuck. We may think that the answer to a particular question or situation is clear, but if others continue to advocate another approach or indicate that they are not happy with ours then there is nearly always something in what they say. It may not appear reasonable to us but their stance or emotion represents something which we need to explore and take account of, if we are to make progress. Even more challenging are those situations when we see and experience both sides. There are no obvious right answers and such situations test our ability to be ourselves and be a part of the group. There are times when we need to contain our 'unsettledness', say and do nothing, and live with the strain of that.

Leaders and groups often avoid the strain of not knowing through a simplistic analysis along the lines of 'they just don't get it'. 'They' will often be the next tier down in the management hierarchy or another rival group. They will be described in general terms as if they were a homogeneous group. Usually there will also be a dose of wishful thinking, as in 'if only they could get it' or 'if they were all like X (a person we like) we would be fine'. This is lazy thinking, and if you are serious about your leadership you cannot afford to be lazy. We all carry the compulsion to divide the world into 'goodies' and 'baddies' and write some people off as 'incompetent', 'stupid', 'political' or 'manipulative'. It's very natural, and it is a trap.

Holding our differences in a group requires us to think about how we hold our conversations. We speak about 'holding' conversations but we don't stop to think about what it means. In fact, it is a critical leadership practice. In Mike's story the team usually cut short conversations in which differences became apparent which held them back from becoming a high-functioning team. If the leader shies away from these critical moments then the team will follow with some relief. Some may want to fight others to smooth it over perhaps, by cracking a joke. In these moments your job as leader is to be settled enough to *hold* the conversation. To insist in some way (which doesn't necessarily mean doing much talking) that the group takes this experience seriously. That this is not glossed over, something important has been opened up, 'let's talk about it'. If you can hold the conversation about your differences long enough there is every chance that something unexpected and new will emerge.

Spotting defensiveness in the group – 'reinventing the wheel'

Groups become very skilled at avoiding things that are uncomfortable and unsettling. In hard-pressed organizations the most immediate priority is likely to be meeting performance targets and 'doing more with less'. In these circumstances it isn't long before someone says 'let's not reinvent the wheel; they have already done this in another part of the organization or elsewhere. Let's do what they do'. This usually prompts agreement and relief around the table, and in that moment we are trapped and condemned to frustration and failure.

If we accept that an organization is a living, social process, not a machine, then context is all-important – the culture and history of the organization, the business situation, the particular individuals and teams you are working with. In other words you are leading while being part of (and in the middle of) an invisible cultural web of connected groups. The groups, or group, that you are working with, large or small, have embedded habits and patterns of working together – 'It's the way things get done around here.' The idea that your organization is like a computer and can take 'best practice applications' from elsewhere and 'plug and play' completely ignores and disrespects this delicate ecology.

Burke reminds us that there is wisdom held by institutions and groups that is the product of long experience but which no one person can readily articulate. People need to come together and talk to surface this wisdom.

Knowing what works well in different parts of the organization (or other organizations) can provide useful data, but we still have to do the work to make it our own. To do otherwise assumes that the only thing that matters about a wheel is that it is round, thereby mistaking a starting point for an end point. Think about how many very different wheels you can immediately call to mind. For hard-pressed leaders this can be difficult to accept, particularly if you tell yourself that all that is happening is 'wheel reinvention'. 'Wheel reinvention' has become a derogatory term suggesting wasted activity. Try telling yourself that the group is using the best evidence and experience to create the perfectly adapted wheel for its particular situation.

Working well with your group – what you can do

Developing trust, loyalty and attachment with groups takes focus and investment. The idealized templates of performing teams and perfect leaders aren't of much use when it comes to the complexities of the here and now and the group of people you actually have. Constant negotiation and adaptation is needed, as people and circumstances change. The key is to 'get real' about yourself and the group. You can only be the leader you can be; and the group can only be the group it can be. If we can accept ourselves enough, if we can accept others enough, then we have the capacity to develop together and be effective. Here are some ideas.

Pay attention to how the group is working. In practice this means:

• Allowing time for people to connect and gossip – and seeing that as part of the 'real' work of the group.

- Acknowledging (late) arrivals and (departures), not to punish or embarrass but to welcome and recognize that when someone leaves a group we are diminished. For example, when someone leaves early say 'Thank you for coming, could you say a word about what you are taking away from this meeting?'

- Pay attention to who is speaking, not speaking and the pattern of communication. Notice when there is, and is not, energy. Sometimes it's as simple as 'Shall we take a break for five minutes?'

- When the group is stuck on a particular task or agenda item be prepared to step in and say 'I notice we seem to be stuck on this, do others feel the same?' Be prepared to follow up with another suggestion such as 'Shall we talk to our neighbour for five minutes about this?'

- Insist that from time to time the group talks about how members are working together; what's helping, hindering and what they appreciate about the group.

- When appropriate be prepared to get tough with the groups:
  ° Seize the moment: when differences and conflict surface encourage the group to stay with it. Say: 'This seems important and I know we all trust each other so let's stay with it for a while.'
  ° If you have a sense that the group has reached agreement too early be prepared to say: 'I think we might be missing something here.'
  ° Tackle defensive behaviour, such as when members of the group blame others who are not in the room (ask: 'What's our part in creating this?') or close down discussion with strategies like 'let's not reinvent the wheel' (ask: 'What are we missing here?').

In relation to each of the significant groups you belong to ask yourself:

- Who's in and who's out of each group? Do others need to be invited or excluded?

- Do we trust each other enough to speak our minds (constructively) and rely on each other?

- How much energy do we have to work together?

- How do I satisfy my need to be significant while serving the group?

- How do we hang on to what's special about this group while adapting as the needs and the group change?

In this complex and shifting world, belonging to a single 'us' is not the whole picture, that's bonkers! We are often working with a range of groups, both inside and outside our primary organization.

In the next chapter we explore working with communities – each of which may contain multiple groups. We address the question 'How do we help connect people with different and conflicting loyalties and help them feel part of something larger?'

CHAPTER 7

Organizations as Communities

'To be attached to the subdivision, to love the little platoon we belong to in society, is the first principle (the germ as it were) of public affections. It is the first link in the seriès by which we proceed towards love to our country and to mankind.'

Edmund Burke, *Reflections on the Revolution in France*

In the previous two chapters we explored what it means to be settled enough and to be able to find yourself in a group – to be yourself as part of something. In this chapter we explore further what that 'something' is. We pursue the idea that organizations can be much more than organization charts and strategies, data and targets, systems and processes. They can be communities; groups of people with shared identities, loyalties, values and commitments. We suggest that fostering the sense of community connection, interdependence and shared culture – 'the way we do things around here' – is part of the critical work of leading. It is not a luxury or an expedient when there is a problem, but a precondition of performance.

We consider what it means to work *in* and *with* organizations as communities.

The sense of being a member of a community is not, of course, a simple thing. Many of us are members of various, overlapping communities. We have different, and sometimes conflicting, loyalties. We encounter many different forms of 'us and them', through which we establish our identity and settle ourselves enough.

First, a story about community and culture.

This saga involves not only the relations between groups within the organization, it also brings in wider social influences that affect us all; the cultural soup within which organizational life takes place. It is a practical exploration of what happens to an organization – how it responds – when the world changes significantly.

The example is a Swiss consulting firm established in 1922 and attached to an educational institution. It had a history of providing training and organizational development services to the whole of the Swiss establishment. Its services included the provision of supervision of mental health and social work institutions. It had been privileged by the Swiss state to be the sole supplier of these services and shared a mindset common to Swiss companies and government that 'Swiss is best for the Swiss and Switzerland'.

However, by the 1990s even the Swiss government could no longer ignore the neo-liberal ideology which was becoming ubiquitous throughout the world. In particular, this meant that there was a need for transparency in dealings between companies and institutions – for financial accountability, for competition to be encouraged and for market forces to be allowed to dictate how and what got done. There was also a growing belief in the importance of evidence-based evaluation of services.

The practical upshot was the opening up to foreign companies of the market for its consulting services. In practice, these companies proved to be the big consulting firms from the USA and UK which were experienced in competing for (and winning) the contracts. While the Swiss firm was well established in the local context, it was relatively small and completely inexperienced in processes of competitive tendering.

The history of the firm over 70 years had led to a culture of over-confidence and blind belief in their superiority. At the same time, silos had built up with each sub-group invested in its own superiority, and there was a divide and rule culture at the top. The management team consisted of the heads of each of the silos coming together in order to divide up work and keep real collaboration to a minimum; 'real collaboration' being akin to treachery and betrayal of each silo's superiority and difference. Only when they really, really had to would the organization come together as a whole. By 1995 they were ripe for being competed out of the market, or taken over; they decided to call in outside help.

When they contracted with us they wanted to reflect on the processes that might be blocking change. The brief included getting to know the underlying fears of change that existed within the organization, and also the different types of connections that existed between all levels of the organization. It also involved bringing in some knowledge about their competitors and how they could learn to compete and so survive.

The work started with an analytically led 'Large Group', held at the top of a mountain in a hotel ballroom which was big enough for all the 120 staff to sit together in a circle of chairs. In analytically led groups, the method is free association and no goal, agenda or task is set. The idea is to surface what needs to be said but is too frightening to express in normal situations in the workplace. The open space in the group, uncluttered by tasks and agenda items, surfaces what is normally hidden.

The group fell into silence, increasing the psychological pressure within the group; something which often leads to someone speaking up about an issue that really matters to them and to others. It was a hot day and the windows were open. As the organization sat and communed in silence, so the sound of all the church bells in the valley came clearly into the old ballroom – marking the fiftieth anniversary of the end of the Second World War in Europe. Someone started crying.

She was sitting opposite me, at the other end of the room. Everyone lowered their heads and looked away from her – preferring to stare into the empty space of the floor in the middle of the group. Only when the bells stopped did people lift their heads. At that point I asked her what the connection was between the sound of the church bells, her tears and the fact that everyone apart from me had avoided looking at her. 'A few months ago,' she answered, 'we had another consultant working with us. As a result around 10 people lost their jobs. I'm crying for them and I'm scared the same thing will happen after today. But I'm also crying because we were spared the suffering of the Second World War . . . I remember my parents being frightened throughout the whole of it . . . they feared being occupied by the Germans . . . But my tears are also for the shame of Switzerland, because of the money that was never returned to the victims of the Holocaust and the fact that we bankrolled some of the Nazi dealings.'

In the conversations that followed it became clear that, while the firm looked complacent, even arrogant, from the outside many inside questioned the way things were working. The firm as a whole needed to shift from a focus on preserving one fixed truth to embracing a way of working that saw learning as the continuing process at the heart of their work. In order to do this they had to re-learn how to connect with the world and each other; they had to get real about what it was they did and what the world expected and needed from them; and they needed to rediscover how to get help from each other. They had to find ways of engaging with the boundaries that existed between the 'us' and 'them' of the internal 'silos' and the hierarchy. They also had to learn how to engage with clients, to adapt and change in their dealings with them so that they could remain valuable in their clients' eyes. Above all, they had to learn to engage in tendering processes, finding a way together to win such competition, and secure their own jobs and standing in the outside community.

The group succeeded in doing these things, but it took eight years! The whole organization met twice a year in the way described and mandated small working parties to address specific issues. All the work was informed by the analytical approach of free association and of expressing thoughts and feelings, which *allowed the organizational community to process the fears and defensive responses that were evoked by the necessary changes they had to embrace, and the various options for change they needed to consider. There were unresolvable tensions of perspective between the different departments that could not be wished away. On the other hand, it was possible to work with these tensions. By naming them and bringing them out into the open, there was a sense of relief and energy and a willingness to grasp the nettle together.*

Naming things for what they are is a powerful and important process in enabling a community to stick together and co-operate beyond their functional and specialist divisions. Naming things aloud and in front of others amounts to a way of ordering and reordering the world we find ourselves in externally, and the world we belong to and identify with internally. The symbolic naming of how we see things does not in itself define the meaning of what is being perceived and said, but it allows members of a group and community to confirm or adapt the meaning of who they are, what they stand for, and why they do what they do.

Through naming things the organization came to behave like a parliament, with groups working on different issues and reporting back to the whole. The management team did work on its own practice, but not as something outside of the other work streams. They behaved as if they were simply another one of the working groups that were all working together to reinvigorate and recreate the organization. So the management team, like any of the working parties, came to the whole organization group with the dilemmas it was facing and invited the wider population to support them in choosing what to do. They assumed that they did not have a monopoly on all the knowledge and wisdom they needed to make a decision – that they couldn't, on their own, know the 'right' answer. From the beginning, the organization was creating collective support for what was being done and the choices that were being made. There was no preaching and no bullying and by the end the organization had a sense of collective community while at the same time nurturing and sustaining healthy sub-group identities within the collective; these sub-groups largely being informed by the variety of professional expertise within the firm.

The organization also became more outwardly orientated, better at staying in touch with external reality. It created a board of governors linked to the needs of the Swiss civil, social, medical and academic services. The firm had changed, but it stayed connected to its roots, its Swiss identity – its new board spoke for Swiss civil society whose servants this firm had always been since its founding in the 1920s. What had changed had been the firm's ability to be attractive in the eyes of Swiss civil society of the twenty-first century. As a last step in the process, the old boss stood down and the next generation took over.

In reading the Swiss story you may be thinking 'we haven't got eight years, we can't afford the time to go on retreat up a mountain every year and free associate; expressing thoughts and feelings would not go down well in my organization'.

We chose this particular story because it highlights, exaggerates even, much that is important about an organization working its way through transformation. Every organization is different. This particular organization chose an approach which was sufficiently consistent with its values, working practices and culture. The Large Group work approach offered this organization a communal space in which the exchanges across departmental and speciality boundaries ended up confirming the group's common social identity, location and psychological security. On this basis the organization and its sub-groups could find the energy for survival and renewal.

At the heart of this story is the idea that, to change in a sustainable way, the various 'us and thems' must find a way to come together as a community with a sufficient common purpose, and must stick with that process long enough for the magic to work. This requires courage from the leadership group because, just like a new kitchen or house extension, these things tend to cost twice as much and take twice as much time as you first thought.

Thinking community

Organizations, just like individuals, survive, thrive, grow and die through existential crises like the one just described. The challenge for leaders is to grasp that such existential questions can only be worked through locally, and that they may take time to address. No amount of PowerPoint presentations will find a shortcut – that will simply drive the process underground. Furthermore, and this may be the hardest step, you cannot control or mandate the process. You have to work with and through it from your own *local* perspective.

The transformation of the Swiss firm began when they came together as a community – bringing their differences into the room with them; not leaving them at the door. We experience, and try to avoid working on, corporate Large Group gatherings which require differences to be left at the door and focus on a superficial unity. This only breeds cynicism. People cannot, and do not, arrive at a common purpose in this way. People need to feel heard before they can engage effectively with other groups and perspectives. In other words, they need to commune together.

People in authority are often nervous about this process for fear it may encourage and amplify division. The temptation is to play down differences to avoid conflict, which can have the effect of reinforcing the silos. However, group and inter-group relationships, identities, purposes and loyalties develop spontaneously. Communities have a life of their own. They grow and decline, are born and die, of their own accord. They do not need to wait for the formal strategies, systems and structures of organizations in order to develop. They can linger long after the formal system has decreed their demise, sometimes as a wound which might reopen during the next restructuring.

These ties and affinities are beyond the control of senior leaders, and the temptation is to view them with suspicion. What's going on? What's cooking up? Will they challenge 'our power and position'? Will they get in the way of 'the change that the organization needs'? By which they usually mean the change 'I have decided on'.

Bringing those at the margins into the centre

Who is to say what change the organization needs? This question takes us to the heart of what it means to think of organizations as communities. If it is not clear already then we should make it clear that we are not advocating the ideas of organization as community as a romantic notion of peace and harmony. The common purpose of effective communities is hard won, and often hard to sustain because it requires a constant process of self and inter-group examination. The community, just like a family, needs to learn how to fall out without falling apart. As the 2016 UK referendum on membership of the EU illustrates, change rarely comes from the centre.

Change often comes from the margins; often from those who are 'getting on with it' while others are worrying about strategies, systems and transformation (as the story of the hospital porters in Chapter 2 illustrates).

Peter Block writes that 'the job of leaders is to invite those at the margins to the centre'. This may sound unrealistic and romantic in today's cut-throat world. In fact it is hugely pragmatic, particularly in complex situations. Paul Uhlig is a heart surgeon who has developed Block's ideas about community in healthcare with the central notion that safe and effective healthcare is an emergent property of a collaborative care team. This stands in sharp contrast to conventional thinking about patient safety which is dominated by management orthodoxy and relies on measurement, checklists, systems, processes and control. Such an approach is mandated from the top and focuses on 'The System'. The unstated assumption behind this approach is that healthcare workers are unreliable and have to be made to deliver safe care by 'The System'. Therefore they need to be inspected and checked on frequently and rigorously.

Uhlig writes: 'The shift from individual leaders to leadership as a collective capability can be puzzling at first. But once it becomes clear that the team itself is the central actor, all sorts of possibilities become available.' Bear in mind that the team membership that Uhlig is referring to is drawn from a whole set of separate silos, all with their own proud tradition – nursing, chaplaincy, pharmacy, portering, cleaning, physicians, physiotherapists, surgeons and so on. He goes on: 'From a collaborative leadership perspective, every role is important and leads at various times. What matters is not who leads, but rather what collaborative leadership accomplishes . . . Collaboration does not mean consensus. It means being able to account for differences while going forward together. Collaborative leadership is authentically curious about multiple viewpoints in appreciative ways.'

An organization doesn't have a culture – it *is* a culture

The Swiss story speaks to a multitude of 'us and thems' and different types of attachments which exist in all organizational settings and every society. The 'us and thems' appear between different levels of the organization, in the connection to (and separation from) the past, and in fearing the future.

The modern, orthodox leadership practice of focusing attention on the future – to a distant transformational change – denigrates the knowledge that people have of past and present. Human beings need to feel safe, secure and settled enough if they are to operate in a mature and adult way. It is these feelings of safety and identity, connected with collective memories of the past, that allow people to take risks, adapt to new conditions and ways without paralysing anxiety. In the madness of modern organizational life, all of this history and experience is swept away. It is labelled as 'the culture', as if it were one inanimate fixed state that exists independently of the organization (and is holding things back). So when leaders assert that 'We need to change the culture' they are seeing it as something separate from them. We think organizations do not have a culture, the organization is a culture. Members of staff live culture in an evolving state, not something fixed or fixable.

Love *your* silo – and build bridges

When working in organizations, we often hear 'We need to break down the silos'. Those at the top of organizations say: 'We need people to take a more corporate view; to stop thinking of their team/department/unit/business/discipline or profession only. We need them to consider the whole organization/company. People must put aside their petty local interests and perspectives, let go of history and look at the bigger picture. We must become one organization. Otherwise we will not succeed (or survive).'

The word 'silo' has taken hold in the organizational world. People are imprisoned, it is argued, in units that don't talk to each other enough, don't consider each other's needs and perspectives, and battle with each other rather than co-operate. They put their own interests first and lose sight of the 'bigger picture'. They are 'not aligned' to the corporate goals and therefore not to be trusted.

Silos are seen as one of the most problematic features of organizational culture that hold back transformational change. The response of orthodox thinking about strategy and change is to attempt to sweep away silos and culture through the magic of redesigning systems, restructuring and appointing a transformational new leader. When this fails, or has unintended consequences, bosses are mystified and usually respond by trying harder, with an even better system, structure and boss. All of this effort is a defence against the anxiety of engaging with the organ-ization as a constant, dynamic, complex, inter-group negotiation between multiple 'us and thems' in search of the glue that holds us all together in a larger community.

We argue that so-called silos are inevitable because belonging to a definable 'little platoon' helps form identity. One person's silo is another person's community. People need to belong, and they cannot work effectively if they do not have the security and susten-ance of being part of a community. The instinct to divide into 'us and them' is normal, as are conflicts and power differences. They can be productive and they can be damaging but it is a hallmark of a democratic society that it has evolved methods of dialogue and dispute resolution that enhance a sense of communal identity and culture. Effective leaders work with the whole organization and its sub-groups in the service of the common purpose, like building cars, combine harvesters, consultancy or banking services.

We therefore argue that leaders need to work in a grown-up way with the differences between silos, not to deny or smooth over or 're-engineer' the differences, as practitioners of the heroic orthodoxy often attempt to do by wanting to reduce the complex-ities of conflicting interest groups within the larger community to 'one firm' or 'one integrated system'. We have seen many attempts to build one organization (like Simon's story in Chapter 3) founder because they are an abstract ideal and don't connect with the experience of people in the organization. What is needed is not to destroy the silos but to build bridges between them. What also helps are ritual gatherings where a sense of community can be experienced, just as a sense of one nation is experienced on the annual Remembrance Day in the UK.

It becomes apparent during such occasions that our sense of community is both a mental construct as well as a felt reality; both are of course not a fixed thing or definition but a reference point for exchanges during which our differences and our common ground can be aired, reaffirmed and, if needed, readjusted. The retelling of old stories on such occasions is not a sign of the organization being frozen in time, but a necessary precondition for dealing with the next adaptive process.

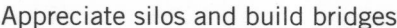

Appreciate silos and build bridges

CEO silos

You too are in your own silo. You may be the CEO but that does not mean that you have superior or special insight into 'the whole' of the organization. Just like everybody else, you have your own *local* perspective that is created within your own silo of the executive team and board. You may be fooled by your position in the hierarchy, the size of your office, the respect that people pay you and so on into thinking that your silo matters more than any others. In certain aspects it does, of course, but that can be true of every other silo too as we quickly discover when, for example, a front-line silo stops co-operating. Each and every silo has its own power and authority. If you can accept that you are in your own silo and recognize your attachment to it then you can also see how destructive (and futile) it is to set out to break down silos.

Through the functioning silo of an executive team you learn about your leadership, become capable of bringing more and more of yourself to the role and develop your leadership authority.

The significance of boundaries

'Us and thems' are created as we create our identity; an emotional process negotiated with and between people, starting in the first 'us' we experience – our family, parents and children. We are who we have become because we carry in us an internalized model of how our family and our kinship system worked. It is the template that helps us make sense of cross-boundary contact, conflict and co-operation in the workplace.

As we have seen, identity and its consequential 'little platoons' are multifaceted and often ambivalent, just like our own kinship system. The way the various sub-groups configure their ambivalent but strong relationships with each other is connected to the formal, rational and hierarchical organization, but also simultaneously grows in the informal network of personal and inter-group relationships, which have their own way of working, rooted in 'the way we do things around here'. This is the world of chance encounters, coffee breaks and corridor conversations. In the kinship system it would have been birthdays, weddings and funerals. In these encounters rumour, gossip and banter are forms of storytelling that create and reinforce our sense of 'us and them'. It is an inherently disordered pattern of interaction.

Often this hidden network of apparently disordered relationships between 'us and thems' orders the work of the whole community. Caldarelli and Catanzaro, in their book *Networks*, write:

'In human societies, social order arises from the combination of autonomous individuals, often with conflicting interests, that still end up performing tasks that nobody could do

on their own . . . Networks, with their emphasis on interactions, are the key to understanding many . . . phenomena. Imagine two football teams whose players have similar skills, and yet the two teams perform very differently: probably this difference depends on how good or bad the interactions are between players on the pitch.'

Keeping your wits about you

If we think of organizations as collections of groups or silos which are constantly shifting, then a leader has a vital part to play in ensuring that the sum of the groups is greater than the sum of the individual parts. They have to ensure that the anxiety engendered by continual reorganizations does not become overwhelming and destroy the capacity of people to work and create together. Leadership is no longer definable in terms of personal qualities and competencies, but by what a leader actually does when faced with a situation where pet answers and standard techniques do not work.

In such critical moments the leader moves from control to co-operation and facilitates the flow of responsibility to the best person and place in the organization. At such moments the leader can be an authority figure and exercise judgement in front of others. They should not try to be the cleverest, but to model that everyone depends on everyone else. The idea of everything depending on the one and only leader is crazy, and in the end counter-productive for the organization.

Leaders as boundary workers

Anthropologists have worked out that when a group encounters another one, they have the tendency to categorize 'us' as belonging to a civilized culture and 'them' as being wild, as yet untamed and a part of nature. This judgement results in concluding that we are more similar than we are, and that others are more dissimilar from us than they are in reality. This creates an 'us and them' which is preserved by maintaining a clear boundary between the two of us. We keep our distance and don't allow them to cross our boundary.

Boundaries have a dual function – they keep things out and let them in. The balance can make a working group effective or ineffective. It is often the role of the leader to operate at the boundary to protect the group enough so that it can be a loyal and committed working group, while linking it with the wider world on which it depends for connectedness, exchange, development, growth, affirmation and survival. The judgement about when to let in other groups and perspectives is critical.

What is needed is to manage the boundaries between different sections, departments and teams to make sure that they don't get locked in to a fixed dynamic of 'us' and 'them', where the focus is not about ability and skill at working together but instead on feeling superior to the other. Real working together, across group identities, requires the leader to focus on freeing up the self-reinforcing stories that groups tell themselves if they are left undisturbed. What conversations, what different voices will help the group see itself as others see it? Our experience has taught us that groups which can deal with difference and cohesion within their own group find it easier to link arms across organizational boundaries, and find others helpful rather than threatening.

So-called 'System Leadership'

'At no time in history have we needed such system leaders more. We face a host of systemic challenges beyond the reach of existing institutions and their hierarchical authority structures. Problems like climate change, destruction of ecosystems, growing *scarcity of water, youth unemployment, and embedded poverty and inequality require unprecedented collaboration among different organizations sectors and even countries. Seeing this need, countless collaborative initiatives have arisen in the past decade – locally, regionally and even globally. Yet more often than not they have foundered – in part because they fail to foster collective leadership within and across the collaborating organizations.'*

Senge et al., 'The Dawn of System Leadership'

Teams, organizations and governments can achieve little on their own. They need to find ways of co-operating with other silos to meet the complex challenges that we face. So far so good.

However, we have also chosen this quotation because it is an example of the flawed thinking that traps us. The authors call for 'System Leadership' to address complex issues, and in this way create the idea of 'system' as something independent and separate from the network of relationships that exists between individuals, organizations and their silos. Just like 'culture', the 'system' becomes a thing that is somehow 'over there' and not embedded and enacted in me and my relationships. Critically, by making the system into a thing in this way, we reduce our power to affect change. This happens because our attention is drawn to fixing or improving 'the system'. If only we could create the perfectly designed system then the world would be perfect – or a lot better at least.

This kind of wishful thinking has led, for example, to UK politicians repeatedly reorganizing the NHS to create a better system. Each reorganization unleashes a whole set of unintended consequences, and just as significantly, reinforces the belief of NHS workers and leaders that they themselves are powerless to do anything to improve the situation because 'it's the system'. We can only imagine what would emerge if (as in the Swiss story) those who want to transform the NHS were able to sit in silence with those who work in it.

Systems thinking served us well in the twentieth century but has been colonized by managers who, as McGilchrist points out, prefer the abstraction of an imagined, fanciful system (how the world *should* be) to real life (the world as it *is*). If we allow ourselves to be drawn into thinking about the system, we are withdrawing from the world and from understanding our part in making it the way that it is.

Working with community – what you can do

If you are interested in exploring what community leadership might mean in your context, then we suggest you read *Community: The Structure of Belonging* by Peter Block. In it he sets out, in practical ways, how this way of leading is radically different. In our experience, the most important shifts required are to:

- **Invite those on the margin into the centre.** Which individuals and groups have you been ignoring and who need to be heard? Personally invite people who are not used to being together; don't leave it to others. Don't mandate or require them to participate but clearly state the *possibility* that the meeting is about to take place and make clear what you hope for from them. Develop ritualized community meetings in which different interests and silos talk and listen, and can identify what they hold dear together.

- **Focus on questions not answers.** Questions, if they are personal and engaging, open the door to possibility and commitment. Develop your capacity to ask powerful and engaging questions. Encourage curiosity about everything including analysis, direction and advice. Ask people, and yourself, 'What have you done to contribute to the very thing you complain about or want to change?' and 'What can you do now?' If we cannot value our own contribution, we are less likely to value that of others.

- **Foster the dialogue that enables people to take responsibility**. Dissent and doubt (not lip service) are needed to open the way for commitment. When dissent surfaces, just listen; don't defend or explain. Use 'open space' methods to surface what people really hope and fear, and to reconnect people with each other and focus on what is most important.

What we have discovered over many years of working with organizations is that, perhaps counter-intuitively, it is by being prepared to consider difference that genuine common ground emerges. It is by taking the risk of facing possible painful disagreement and conflict, by listening and showing respect, that dangerous conflicts can turn into fruitful sources of difference. People can see if what unites is more important than what divides them.

Ultimately, individuals lead well when they come to terms with the reality that the communities they are leading temporarily are more important than them. They become most effective when they realize that their leading is not about them but what they – their character, their strengths and weaknesses, their beliefs and values – represent for others, in the communities they work with.

Perhaps elected politicians know this well. They appreciate that their position is fragile, temporary and subordinate to the will of the people. They know that, imperfect as it may be, democracy matters more than their position or party. They recognize that the point of party politics is to struggle for power and to be in power. We can think of organizations as communities, but most are not in any sense a democracy. Perhaps that's why many of us find organizational politics hard to take, and we explore this in the next chapter.

CHAPTER 8

Politics and Power

There is what is right in the world and there is what is real. Effective leaders operate at the intersection of the two.

We meet many people in organizations who have an ingrained aversion to organizational politics. They see politics as divisive, sinister and illegitimate. They say: 'Without politics, this organization would function smoothly.' Politics for them is the sand clogging the smooth running of the engine. They are wary of the competition for jobs, status and power which often leads to dishonesty and manipulation. They fear that political skill is incompatible with personal authenticity or professional competence. They report that they have experienced self-serving individuals who pursue their own careers at the expense of others and the organization. They often use politics as a dirty word to describe the bad practices of others. They say: 'I try to do an honest job, but I am not sure about them – they play politics.'

Many professionals split the world into good experts and bad politicians. The dependence of experts and politicians on each other for resources, sufficient power and community support is denied and smothered under a blanket of idealism. A utopian vision is offered of organizational life that is free of conflict, differing interests and the rich plurality of sub-groups that make any community or organization unique and worth living and working in.

We recall one successful company chairman who often berated others for being 'political' – by which he seemed to mean being underhand or dishonest in some way. It was ironic. We admired the chairman not least because we viewed him as politically adept; he would not have risen to be chairman if he had not been. By 'politically adept' we mean he had gained the support of key individuals and groups. He had made skilful reference to shared interests, ideas and sense of identity. He had set out his vision and got in tune with others' hopes and dreams. Coalitions developed to support his rise to the top; some of his own making, some emerging spontaneously. He had used his own sense of authority and the way in which he engaged with people to earn respect and trust; and to allow him to gain positional power in the organization.

In this chapter we offer a different view of politics. We suggest that politics in organizations is unavoidable. Whether you like it or not, handling the politics is part of what we do as leaders – in the sense that politics is the struggle for power and position in and across organizations. At a time when professional politicians are widely regarded with contempt, this may seem strange. Value organizational politics? You can't be serious?

Well yes, we can. We argue that politics is part of seeing organizations as they are – complex, living communities with histories, cultures and dynamics of their own. It is also part of recognizing people as they are – wonderful, inspiring, maddening, ambitious (often) for self as well as for the organization or a valued cause. Instead of denying or defining politics as evil, we believe it would be better to recognize that politics exists and find decent ways of working with it, of making a positive difference.

More than that, we suggest that politics can be an honourable activity. There is, we suggest, a widespread problem with authority in organizations. People in senior positions often do not have much legitimacy in the minds of employees and stakeholders. As the boss you usually have the power to say 'no'. You can stop things happening, you can veto appointments, you can prevent people having a budget. Staff will probably go along with what you say – and that is the challenge. How do you shift from 'people going along' or complying with what you want to prompting the commitment that you need for your organization, team or unit to be successful? How do you enable others to say 'yes', and mean it?

Our experience is that effective leaders, whether consciously or not, work with the politics of their organizations. As we have described previously, they gather together groups committed to certain causes or individuals. They recognize the importance of feelings and emotions, the need for people to belong, to identify with things bigger than themselves. They know the power of uniting together against a common adversary. They understand the importance of fostering a sense of hope and the powerful role that fear can play in groups and organizations.

If organizations are living entities with minds of their own, then it is time to make politics respectable again – and think how to work with it productively.

Politics as assembling working majorities

The need for a decent politics is not a theoretical or abstract point. Hannah Arendt and others, who had direct experience of the collapse of civilized society in mid-twentieth-century Europe before and during the Second World War, saw politics as a vital and honourable calling. If decent people don't step forward, the demagogues and fanatics will. One of Edmund Burke's better-known sayings is that 'All that is necessary for evil to triumph is that good men do nothing'. In an age when the reputation of politics and politicians is so low, never has this been truer.

Scarred by her experience of the Nazis and the Holocaust, Arendt pointed out what happens when decent, thoughtful politics collapses – people are seduced by charismatic leaders who appeal to people as an undifferentiated mass. People stop thinking, abandon their conscience and are prepared to commit murder in order to comply with an abusive leader's wishes or inhuman bureaucratic rules. Sociologist Ralf Dahrendorf argued that politics is an honourable calling, as contempt for it plays into the hands of those who want to abuse both democracy and its citizens. It is therefore vital to have good enough processes for working out conflicting interests and perspectives. It is a sign of a mature society and institutions that they can make considered judgements and choices about controversial issues, and that they do not fall into simple-minded scapegoating and two-dimensional perspectives. A decent politics holds together the tensions in an organization, as in society, and allows them to be productive by finding workable compromises, so that they do not spill over into violence and destruction.

We suggest that politics can be concerned with legitimizing authority – finding a basis for decisions and actions that is acceptable to most people. Politics should seek ways to represent and reconcile different viewpoints and interests. The job of a politician in a liberal democracy is to build a 'working coalition' that enables them to hold power and act for the community as a whole. Similarly, in an organization, the job of a leader can be to develop a working majority that legitimates their power. Getting complex things done involves politics.

One of the challenges of living in liberal democratic countries is that 'we don't know what we've got till it's gone'. We take for granted open debate, the rule of law and checks and balances on the powerful. Sometimes these come into focus when they are threatened; for the most part we don't really notice them.

When we stand back we see that liberal democracy is a relatively recent development. In the western democratic tradition it goes back to the development of government by consent in the seventeenth and eighteenth centuries, which demonstrated what was then a revolutionary idea that far from being weak and divided, government by consent could preserve the order and security of citizens, and indeed be stronger and more durable than dictatorships.

In the last 40 years the need for a civilized politics has got lost again as the heroic orthodoxy has become supreme. If the dominant picture is one of the individual as an economic actor and consumer, making choices in a free market, and there is 'no such thing as society', to quote Margaret Thatcher, then there is not much call for politics. Most choices can be made by market mechanisms. We disagree. Free markets are a theoretical idea. In reality, few markets are completely free; they are shaped by the institutions and cultures that surround them. There is the vital question of who sets the rules for the market – what and how shapes who will be winners and who losers. Extreme free market theorists have not yet succeeded in abolishing the clash of interests and ideas. We still need mechanisms for mediating and resolving those conflicts. In a time of scarcity, we need ways to make choices about who and what should have priority.

Within organizations too there is a need for grown-up processes to recognize and work with different interests and perspectives; a need to help people express what matters to them most; to help them think together about difficult choices; to help them avoid play-acting and attend to the dilemmas and challenges an organization faces; and to draw attention to the purpose and reason for being of organizations.

The central theme is the need to avoid splitting the world into good and evil. How do we live with the idea that we all have a dark side within us – selfish, greedy, anxious, fearful or complacent? Can we accept the insecurity that leads to ambition and a need to be recognized? We all are at risk of projecting on to others dark thoughts that we have about ourselves. Can we tolerate our own dark side? See it as a source of energy and wonder? And not seek to deny or run away from it?

We have to allow for personal ambition. Who in senior positions is not ambitious? Not many. We have to allow for human weakness, our own and others'. In order to get things done, we have to make political alliances. Not as a last resort but as a precondition for success.

Recently, in Europe and the United States, we have seen well-established assumptions about liberal democracy called into question. It is worth remembering that in 1787, 55 men (it was the eighteenth century!) came together in the heat and humidity of summer in Philadelphia to devise a constitution for the new country that had emerged from a desperate war against the British. The 13 states were riven with conflicts, not least about whether to be slave-owning or not, what sort of government was needed and how to hold together in a hostile world. Over the coming weeks, locked together and barred from talking to the press, they hammered out together not just a constitution but a workable model for governing a country of unprecedented size and potential which has lasted to a remarkable degree (whatever the problems) till today.

How did they do it? They were all men soaked in the ideas of government by consent articulated by John Locke and others after the Glorious Revolution in Britain. Until the British government managed to alienate them in the 1760s and 70s, 'Americans' had thought of themselves as free-born and English (with freedom of religion and conscience and limited government) who happened to live on the other side of the Atlantic. Perhaps most importantly, they all had experience of some self-government and of the rough and tumble of debate and negotiation in the colonial state assemblies. Getting business through, negotiating, reconciling different interests and needs – all was second nature to most of them. They were deeply practical, confronted by an urgent and immense task.

Based on their experience they devised a scheme of great subtlety – for example, on how to constitute the federal government with a president like an elected king for a limited period, a senate to represent the states equally and a house of representatives like the House of Commons. Of course, huge controversies (and a civil war) lay ahead. But how many other eighteenth-century institutions have lasted so well? With good reason the meeting has been called the 'Miracle at Philadelphia'.

An Anglo–Dutch merger

A *few years ago we worked with a leading international law firm, led from the Netherlands and the UK, which had come together from the merger of a number of firms. The firm grew in a few years from having some 50 partners to having 550; it faced formidable challenges in bringing together the best of the very different conditions, training, experience and culture of the Dutch and British firms. The British firm was concentrated in London and based on City work; the Dutch firm was devolved across the Netherlands and worked with a much broader range of industries and clients.*

The senior partners of the firm recognized each other as senior elite lawyers, highly paid and used to working with the leaders in business and government. At the same time, there were some sharp differences in the cultures and histories of the firms. Dutch partners struggled sometimes with the indirect ways of speaking of the English. London-centric English partners struggled with the spread of business and government in the Netherlands. There were different patterns of professional education and training. People might speak good business English, but behind the shared words were often very different assumptions.

The firm made the decision to set up a dual Anglo–Dutch leadership to run the firm after the merger. This went against conventional wisdom which says that in a merger one side is bound in due course to come out on top, and it is better to recognize that. It was clear to leaders of the firm that the Dutch partners would not accept being subordinate to the British firm (nor the British to the Dutch). There would have to be a genuine alliance of the two sides.

There was also a long history in both firms of identifying leaders through conversations among leading partners, and not by a process of headhunting to an abstract brief. It was decided to have two leading partners at the top of the firm; one from the

Dutch side and one from the British side. In parallel, each area of practice would also have a British leader and the Dutch leader.

There was another complication. On the Dutch side two firms had previously come together, one with a strong culture of working with the largest firms in Holland and another one used to working with smaller enterprises, but with a strong entrepreneurial mentality focused on growth. It therefore turned out that the leaders in each practice area often turned out to be a trio, one from each of the former Dutch firms alongside a British partner who often ended up mediating between the two Dutch.

Inside the pairs and trios there were robust discussions about priorities and ways of working. It was not possible simply to choose one tradition over another. It was necessary to work through the differences and examine what would help the whole firm for the future. Gradually the leaders who emerged across the firm were those who cared about the success of the new firm as a whole.

We worked with a mini 'parliament' of 50 leading partners, selected from across the firm, to meet once a quarter to guide the development of the firm. As one of the leading partners said: 'You enabled us to talk about the things that mattered.' The partners were sociable. They went on skiing holidays and visited the theatre together. Yet they needed outside support and challenge to help them tackle uncomfortable issues such as the distribution of profits and requests to some partners to leave the firm.

One member of the representative group became notorious with the senior partners for being an awkward customer. He acted, they said, like a 'trade union representative'; he put on the table thorny issues such as how to deal with pensions and under-performers. Over a period, working with this 'awkward' partner proved to be of great value. He became in effect a 'community liaison officer', bringing the issues that ordinary partners were concerned about to the fore and helping to achieve a resolution.

Dual leadership continued for five years until the financial crash. At that point it was decided to have one leader, and a UK partner was elected to the top job.

The process in the law firm was very different from the conventional, top-down ways of driving through change illustrated in Chapter 2. This process involved a careful process of building enough agreement among the group of senior partners and pragmatically finding a way forward to deal with pressing issues. It required open and direct conversations about a number of tough issues.

The lawyers did not come with a grand plan. They recognized in a pragmatic way the constraints they were dealing with and worked it out as they went along. They worked more democratically and consciously in a pluralistic fashion to handle conflicting interests and viewpoints. Instead of simplifying the problem or looking to a magical leader to sort everything out, leaders in the firm moved forward carefully, step by step.

The importance of social capital

The story makes the case for investing in the social capital of your community. It illustrates the importance of helping an organization to work as a community, working with dissent and cultural diversity rather than dismissing its significance by preaching 'one family' or 'one firm' – as if the one community did not have meaningful sub-divisions. Only when dissent and difference is invited into the dialogue can an organizational community move on from simply reacting and solving problems to creating and evolving a joint future together. Politics is then in the service of getting things done on behalf of the organization as a whole.

Organizational politics and leading is not just about being a good boss; it's also about being a good subordinate, and a good citizen of a living community. Yes, hierarchy matters, but not simply in the sense of being in charge at all times. Leading professionally and politically in an organization is a matter of judging when to give a lead, when to leave people to do their work, when to step back and listen, and when to join in with an equal voice. It is a matter of working flexibly with the management of the order of things and simultaneously engaging with individuals, groups, whole communities and outside agencies and partners, across status boundaries and other divisions. It is also to do with recognizing that your organization does not have a culture but is an evolving cultural body that needs due care and attention, not repeated re-engineering attempts.

The law firm recognized that the merged organization brought three very different ways of working, thinking and doing things together, and that tolerance, time, patience and cultural and historical wisdom were needed to resist abstract attempts to make 'one firm' out of the three sub-groups. The leaders took the political risk of being lambasted in the legal press about what they ought to do. They held enough frank discussions in order to arrive at a compromise solution, which could be tested out and financed without too much damage to the business and the newly formed community. These leaders thought politically, acted strategically and communicated with social and psychological awareness and sensitivity.

How it works – political leadership in practice

A powerful finding of our research for our *Living Leadership* book was the focus of successful leaders on managing upwards. As we said then, 'the pressure for short-term results, the sense of overload and . . . Constant changes in people and organization have led to many leaders being preoccupied with looking for security in attaching upwards to those who seem to have power.' The preoccupation with managing upwards can be productive or it can be damaging. It can be at the expense of engaging well with people's own teams and the rest of the organization. We some-times saw followers who were delighted to sit back and leave responsibility with the leader. Implicitly they were saying to their leader: 'You're the hero, you're paid all this money, you get all this attention . . . You do it.'

It is therefore important to find ways of managing upwards that are not at the expense of relationships with your own team or people. Here is one example.

Gordon's story

Gordon was the newly appointed managing director of the UK division of a US manufacturing company. The previous boss had been sacked. Head office in America felt he had been too slow to move on the competitive challenges faced by the division. The division was still making money, but there was a sense that it was living on borrowed time. Low-cost competition from the Far East was eroding its position. Action was needed quickly if the division was to survive more than a few years ahead.

Gordon had worked for the corporation most of his career. He knew the big bosses in the States well and had a strong link with the chief operating officer, who had once been his boss at another division. Gordon's natural style was consultative. He believed deeply in taking people with him. A private and thoughtful man, with a strong interest in strategy, he was also very unassuming and approachable. He was a loyal company servant who on several occasions had been prepared to uproot his family to move to new posts around the company.

Gordon did not know the business he was coming into. He had worked for the corporation around the world in a number of divisions, but never before in this particular sector. Members of the executive team he inherited were sceptical. They were worried about the intentions of head office and knew of Gordon's links to the COO. Was Gordon going to be the COO's hatchet man?

Early on, Gordon decided to involve not just the executive team but other managers in defining the challenge that the company faced and deciding what to do. One manager in the executive team was almost openly hostile. He asked how a strategic review would help. The problems, he said, were well known. It was time to act. Other members of the executive team were unenthusiastic but nevertheless willing to be involved. It looked as if they were taking their time to get the measure of the new boss.

Gordon established a number of small groups looking at different strategic issues – customer needs and wants, internal competencies, supply chain, product development. The small groups each included a mix of managers from different functions and levels. Outside consultants were only used to help with the process and not with the content of the work.

At first the work started slowly. Gordon felt discouraged. He organized a meeting of all the work groups – about 20 people in total – but the energy seemed low and people reluctant to take the initiative. However, within a few weeks people began to report progress. Managers found that important data and insights were available but had not been shared because the previous boss never thought to involve people in the strategy. Managers relished the chance to look at things from a company, not just functional, perspective. We also guessed the managers were beginning to feel that Gordon was 'for real' – that the process was not a sham and that Gordon was really listening. Gordon asked very good questions and he did seem determined to get different perspectives on the issues.

All the time, Gordon was receiving phone calls from the COO, asking him when he was going to close the UK factory and move production to China. The COO was a powerful figure, very clever and ambitious. He knew the answer. Our view was that it took some courage from Gordon to push back and say that he needed more time to decide what was right. It also seemed clear that Gordon could not have pushed back if he had not had a strong relationship with the COO.

After three months the work groups came together for another two-day meeting. This time the atmosphere was very different. Engaged and energized, the managers participated in passionate discussion. Despite protests from the marketing director, Gordon insisted on inviting some customers in to hear 'from the horse's mouth' what was most important to them. It became clear that the company wasn't doing enough to meet customer needs. There was a great opportunity to improve service. Managers became enthusiastic as a pattern emerged – the same issues and possible ways forward had emerged from several work groups. What was previously unspoken was now firmly on the table for everyone to deal with.

It became clear that the case for moving to China did not add up at that moment. The challenges of providing prompt service to meet different customer needs across Europe were too great, and the cost of transport from China too high. In the medium term, production would remain in the UK.

Six months later the COO asked Gordon to replace the boss of another, larger division, who had suddenly died. With regrets for 'a job half done', Gordon moved on.

In difficult circumstances, Gordon managed his boss with great courage and insight. He knew how his boss thought, the clarity of thinking that was required, and the need to provide good data at every step. He kept his boss closely informed and supplied the facts and analysis that were required. At each stage he did not ask the COO for the impossible. He asked for time and for the evidence to ensure that decisions were well founded. He could not have done it without a strong, pre-existing relationship with the boss.

At the local level too Gordon was capable. He did not spend too much time trying to convert the manager who was cynical about the whole exercise. He invested in working with the people who were amenable to his approach. He played to his natural style, which was to involve people and seek to build agreement.

He took his time and knew from experience how long the development of the strategy would take. He was prepared to dig in on key issues such as inviting in customers. Intuitively, he had an eye, the whole time, to winning a working majority among the managers in the company.

Gordon succeeded because of his close relationship with both the COO and his own team. When he spoke with the COO he was increasingly speaking on behalf of his team and company. He was not on his own, facing power, but representing something bigger than himself. He avoided the trap that we see many fall into of seeking to manage upwards, on his own, thereby becoming overly fearful and compliant. He broke with the myth that is part of the heroic orthodoxy – that it is all up to the leader. Gordon won authority with and for others.

Speaking truth to power

Our colleagues, Megan Reitz and John Higgins, have researched when and how people feel able to speak 'truth to power'. They have explored both when we feel able to speak openly with those who are more powerful than us, and how we influence those around us to speak (or not speak) their truth to us.

Reitz and Higgins conclude that it is not a simple matter of exhorting individuals to have courage. They draw attention to the way in which these phenomena are 'co-created' by individuals and groups in specific contexts. It's not very effective to ask individuals to set a different pattern on their own. There has to be some support from the organization and from those around them. Reitz and Higgins focus particularly on developing judgement, in context; to know when and how to speak more openly.

In Sophocles' drama *Oedipus the King*, another version of truth-telling is explored. When the community is 'sick', the King calls in the blind truth-seer, in the belief that the one who cannot see will not turn a blind eye to what is really going on. The old truth-seer is ready to die and has nothing to lose. Consequently, he is free to say that the King himself is the primary source of the sickness in the body politic.

It is the person in authority who ultimately pays the price if people cannot speak 'truth to power'. It is they who do not hear what is really going on, and what they need to pay attention to if they are to survive. It therefore pays a modern leader to facilitate political processes for truth-saying, upwards and downwards.

Balancing power

Power is a matter of what you believe about yourself, and whether others choose to have confidence in you. Why are some people more powerful than others? We are often struck that some people *choose* to be powerful. They tell themselves a story in which they have power and influence. Others, in similar positions, tell themselves a story of being powerless. In other words, some leaders are over-confident about power and others are under-confident. What is clear to us is that power and authority are always dependent on context and the network of relationships in which a particular leader is located. The heroic orthodoxy tends to suggest that only autocratic forms of the exercise of power are effective. We suggest that a more participative and democratic use of power in organizations, congruent with the values and ideals we cherish in society, is less wasteful and more effective.

To return to Tillich, whose ideas we drew on in Chapter 5, power is 'the drive of everything living to realize itself, with increasing intensity and extensity'. 'Realizing itself' – whether we are talking about an individual, group or community – is necessary if we are to achieve our potential. However, if realizing ourselves is all we do, it becomes selfish and divisive; so it needs to be balanced with love, which Tillich defines as 'the drive towards the unity of the separated', or community, as we described in the previous chapter. As Adam Kahane explores in his book *Power and Love*, leaders in particular have to choose *both* power and love. In many ways holding these things in balance is what politics is all about. It is having the insight and intelligence to judge: If I exercise power by pushing ahead with this initiative, is the community (or love) strong enough to support the development?

Working well with politics and power – what you can do

Fortunately we are not all-powerful and so we cannot bend the world to our will. We have to be ambitious and realistic about the scope we have to influence or shape events. What is the art of the possible? What can we do, here and now, to have an effect? How can we do this with integrity?

Understand *your* power and authority

In our work we often support leaders in receiving verbatim '360 feedback' from people they work with. We find that leaders are surprised by their authority with others. They are surprised to learn that others follow them not because of speeches or PowerPoint presentations but because they embody values, principles or objectives for others.

How aware are you of your sources of authority with others? There are many different kinds. Talk with your group and others about when they find you at your most powerful. How can you make the most of the person you are? As we described in Chapter 5, this goes hand in hand with the work to find a settled enough self. Be kind to yourself and keep in good enough shape to lead others.

Don't give your power away unintentionally

We all find ways of giving our power away. Sometimes it's as simple as overplaying a real strength so that it becomes a weakness. Find the 'micro-habits' that make you less effective. This can be as straightforward as saying too much or too little, as well as how we present ourselves, or whether we smile and make eye contact.

In today's organizations the number of skilled intelligent people who think of themselves as powerless is remarkable. This is partly the result of the heroic orthodoxy that tells people that it is all up to the one great leader at the top. It is also a matter of choice and life history. We disempower ourselves with our old stories of 'not belonging, not being good enough or being found out'. These stories let us off the hook because we free ourselves of responsibility for what we can do and settle back into blaming others. They don't make us effective leaders.

Understand and appreciate the power distribution that surrounds you

You may tell yourself 'I don't do politics', but that's naïve. Others will see your actions as political. In order to anticipate the likely impact of your actions you need to have a sense of the 'power map' of which you are part. Who has power and influence, above and below? Who do you have good relationships with? Who are you prepared to work with? It may help to literally sketch out this 'power map' for yourself.

Imagine yourself in the shoes of the bosses. What is the context for them? What are the pressures on them? What are their needs and objectives? What are their hopes and fears? Are you prepared to see your bosses as ordinary mortals (not devils or heroes) and consider how the world looks to them? Are you able to be curious and explore their interests and views (and not judge or condemn)?

Whatever your context, you are likely to have some operational 'box ticking' as part of your normal work. Don't do it out of hours and resent it, or do it badly because you are angry about it. It may be a necessary, if maddening, part of what you do. Meeting these requirements is part of power and politics.

Grow power by connecting your story to others'

It is easy to imagine that power is finite and that we gain more by taking it from others. This may be true of coercive 'power over' others, but it is not so with the 'power to' which comes from creating possibilities, by being part of something, with others.

Think about the benefits to others and to the organization of the things that you and your group are trying to achieve. Listen and enquire, don't sell. Develop some shared ground. How can you develop the necessary relationships *and* business justifications?

As we discussed in Chapter 4, strategy is a constantly shifting story. How could you make a contribution and develop the story? Instead of being compliant or complaining, how could you fill in part of the picture? What groups or interests do you identify with and/or want to support?

See politics as balancing self- (and common) interest

Chief executives are not elected by employees. Nevertheless, the principles of liberal democracies – the rule of law, open debate, limits on the power of any one individual and mechanisms for finding working majorities for change – need to play out in organizations as in society as a whole; power and love working together.

The authority to lead is not something given from above; it is negotiated, day by day, between people as they work together. Winning the support of a working majority is not something to be put off to some imagined future that will never arrive. It is something that, step by step, we can implement in our own world.

Power, politics and group dynamics play out in every meeting we join; there is so much going on that is not on the agenda. In many ways the simplest of meetings is unfathomable. Perhaps that's why meetings are denigrated.

If you take yourself seriously as a leader, you cannot afford to play this game. Meetings do matter, and you need to make them productive, which is what we consider in the next chapter.

CHAPTER 9

Making Meetings Productive

There are some things that we don't hear as organization consultants. For example: 'The problem with our board is that we spend too much time on strategy and not enough on finance.' Or, 'Since I became a director, I find I have much more time on my hands.'

Surprising as hearing those statements would be, it would be truly shocking to hear 'I love meetings so much I just don't have enough to go to.'

Can your meetings be more than a joke?

Meetings are the universal bane of organizational life, and the subject of much mockery. We have attended our share of horror shows; meetings that seem confused, energy sapping and pointless – and some that are laughably inept.

Such meetings may include some (or even all) of the following:

- People are not properly introduced – you don't know the other people in the room or what their role is with regard to the subjects under discussion.

- The topics to be discussed are not clear or well framed – why are you discussing this today? What is the objective?

- Agendas are stuffed with items – there is far more to talk about than can ever be dealt with properly in the time available.

- People work through a standard agenda without reference to an issue or issues that people are crying out to address.

- People talk but don't make clear what they are really saying.

- Conclusions and next steps are not clear – people leave with different impressions of what was discussed and what, if anything, was decided.

In many places the experience is repeated in the same meeting week after week. We all join the meeting knowing how it will go. We dare not miss it, however, because it is axiomatic that 'if you are not at the table, you are on the table'.

How bonkers is that?

And then there is the dark side of meetings. Primitive feelings are stirred in us – insecurities about whether we belong or not; anxieties about being excluded; and fears of being exposed or shamed in front of a group. Many of us have gone to meetings with the primary purpose of subverting the supposed purpose of the session in order to avoid taking on more work or to fend off decisions. These problems have been made worse by the explosion of 'virtual' meetings over the phone and internet. How familiar is this story?

I was one of seven people around the country attending a telephone conference. We logged in in good time and waited for the chairman, Frank, to arrive on the call. After some text and email queries, we heard that Frank had meant to be in Manchester but that his train was delayed.

After about 20 minutes he came on the line. He said that the issue was important and time was pressing so he wanted to go ahead with the meeting. He tried to lead the discussion from his mobile phone. We heard a running commentary and background noises as his train approached Manchester and then as he sat in a taxi on his way to an office. Along the way Frank challenged two of the participants on the call, asking what they were doing to move forward the subject under discussion. Unfortunately, while he was doing this, his mobile signal cut out. We heard the irritating message, 'Frank has left the conference'.

Eventually, Frank gave up and said he would reconvene the group on another date – but not before seven very irritated people had wasted an hour and a half of their time and a great deal of goodwill.

What we often hear is: 'I have to go in early or stay late because it is only at the start and end of the day (or at the weekend) that I can get any work done. The rest of the time I am in meetings.' Notice the separation – meetings are *not* work, they are, well, meetings. What's going on? Why do we persist with apparently pointless meetings? And why are effective meetings not more common?

Our experience is that people often don't see the opportunity to change the way meetings play out. They tend to see meetings as a force of nature, something that happens *to* them, not something they can shape. 'It's the second Tuesday in the month so it must be the meeting of the management committee' they say. 'But what is the purpose of this meeting? What are *you* trying to achieve in this session?' we ask. 'Not sure, I'll have to think about that.'

We also observe many people who fail to allow for proper preparation and follow-up. We can think of very capable senior leaders who, because they're clever, think that they can 'wing it'. Sometimes they get away with it. At other times they fall flat on their faces.

In this chapter we suggest that meetings don't have to be horror shows. Meetings can be business-like and encouraging. They can be fit for a wide range of purposes, provided, of course, you are clear enough about what your purpose is!

Meetings are places where the drama of your organization plays out. Leaders can use them to influence culture and performance, to help their people achieve what is most important.

Here's a story of one leader who changed the way meetings worked for her and her group.

Isobel's story

One of us shadowed Isobel in one of her weekly team meetings. During the meeting Isobel asked her coach to offer feedback, not just on her performance but on the way the group had worked. The coach outlined some of the patterns he had noticed in the group. He highlighted the very full agenda of the meeting. Then he asked team members to offer their views. The team members revealed that they were inhibited from working well because the leader spoke to each individual in turn and not to the group as a whole. The person on the spot felt pressurized and the rest withdrew into the role of spectator and apparently innocent bystander who feels slightly ashamed of not correcting the picture drawn by the leader.

Isobel decided to change the agenda for the next meeting. She reduced the agenda from 20 down to three items. When this business had been done, she asked the team and the coach to explore openly and without fear what prevented the team working more effectively and creatively together and apart. She handed the role of facilitator over to the coach. A discussion ensued about how to get the best from the group. It became clear that everyone was guilty of telling the leader what they thought she wanted to hear. The messages ran along the lines of 'everything is fine'; 'we have no problems'; 'all the work is on track'. The leader colluded with this pattern of dialogue because she did not invite 'problematic news' and also neglected to invite the rest of the team to explore what they heard. The coach then asked four of the presenters from the previous meeting to tell the story of their current work again, outlining the good news but also revealing what was not going so well. Having done that, they were invited to ask a colleague with relevant knowledge to give some advice.

This led to a significant shift in the way that Isobel led and the way she related to her team. A new deputy was appointed, a new structure and new roles set in place. Isobel started to trust more and let go of holding too many matters in her own hands. She gave her team more responsibility for day-to-day decision making and the team told her that they valued her strategic role. Her time and energy was freed up to do more of her own work and to take more part in the leadership of the organization. She was able to live the strategic part of her role more openly and effectively.

Isobel's authority with the group shifted. She moved from fear to trust; from trying to rule over the group to building a working relationship with each person. Members of the group were more able to help each other, and help Isobel take responsibility. Isobel made more differentiated judgements about her people as it became clear that two members of the team were struggling. Some members of the team could take on more responsibility and some could not. Isobel listened over a wider range; she started to notice danger signs from individuals, some of which had been hidden before. Isobel turned her attention to anticipating problems that individuals might have, and seeking to address them. She moved, as it were, from therapeutic to preventative medicine.

Often the issue for leaders is 'Where do I start? I know I can't tackle everything, but what should I tackle now?' In this case, tackling the way Isobel's team meetings were run proved to be a good enough place to start. Change came from disturbing existing patterns. Isobel was keen to experiment – not talk about it but do it!

Isobel was courageous; willing to open up issues without knowing for sure where it would lead. And she was capable, with a sure grasp of the business the team had to do and an intuitive sense of people and the dynamics in the room. The timing was right and the group ready to move. Intelligent opportunism paid off.

Culture changes one meeting at a time

This story illustrates that every time we meet with a group we have an opportunity to influence culture, the 'way things are done around here'. We are not only doing the task that is needed, we are influencing the social fabric, reinforcing current norms or causing them to shift. Whether we recognize it or not, we have a choice. Often we may decide we don't want to offer a lead, that it is not that important and that there is no realistic chance of moving things in the way we think is needed. It is your choice. If you decide not to intervene in a meeting that frustrates you then you will need to find another way of accommodating that frustration, so that you don't become a victim of it.

However, when it is important to us and we do have influence, then the potential is there. To be influential, we have to recognize that this is emotional as well as intellectual work. We cannot control what goes on, but we can be more alert to the signals of what is happening in a group, in the organization and the culture they are part of. Timing is critical as things move on, and the moment passes quickly. We need to use all our antennae and lean on our colleagues and friends to work out what is happening and how to respond. It does not have to be a clever intervention, and you don't need to know 'the answer'. Often it is enough to say something intuitive such as 'Can we stop for a minute and talk about what just happened?' or 'I am feeling uncomfortable and I'm not sure why.' It is by acknowledging our interdependence with others that we become more successful leaders, and more effective in shaping meetings.

Common dysfunctional patterns in meetings

If you are to challenge and change the culture of a specific meeting, it helps if you can spot the dysfunctional patterns that are getting in the way. Here are some examples you may recognize.

'Let's get down to business'

An understandable, if dysfunctional, way of reducing the complexity of meetings is to say things like 'let's just get on with it' or 'let's just be practical and avoid too many intellectual discussions'. The emphasis is on action and doing. Those aspects of meetings that have to do with being human, creative and emotionally enough engaged to want to work hard are neglected.

Scapegoating individuals

There is a tendency to *locate problems in individuals,* who are seen as making mistakes, failing to perform or who do not understand. An alternative view is that the person being blamed represents a problem which belongs to everyone. Leader and group move from wanting to sort out this one person to facing up to how everyone is involved in creating and maintaining the problem. It is a shift from what have *you* done wrong to what have *we* not paid attention to? What can each person in the group do to find a way forward? In that way, the group avoids scapegoating and fosters group cohesion and shared ownership of the problem.

Of course, sometimes (though this is more exceptional than is commonly assumed) the individual really is the problem. The leader then needs to confront the individual in private. They also need to let the group know, publicly, that 'you are carrying some-one else's load' and that the situation will be confronted and made more equitable again. If that is not done, the group can sink into resentment.

'You're the boss'

In many meetings the members of the group act as if they have met to be directed and protected by its imagined powerful, all-knowing leader. In such a meeting the leader feels that they are doing all the work and falls back on telling people what to do. In response the group sinks into passive aggression and asks defen-sive questions such as 'What do you want us to do? Just tell us.' In such moments it is important that the leaders stop themselves from taking over; they need to stay curious, asking things like: 'What are your thoughts and ideas?' Break the collective stance of dependency by addressing specific question to individuals, espe-cially the disengaged ones.

Splitting the world into good and bad

The group may want to identify goodies, baddies, victims and perpetrators. The exchanges will be marked by sentiments such as 'they are to blame'; 'it's not our fault'; 'it's all too much'; and 'What can we do, except sit it out and let it pass?' In the grip of such thought patterns the group loses its capacity for empathy and thoughtful dialogue.

Fight or flight?

Splitting the world in this way invites the group to fight with the baddies, or run away and ignore the situation. Under pressure to join in the game, a leader (or a thoughtful group member) can break the spell of this temptation by asking: 'What is it in me that tempts me into simplifying this story into goodies and baddies? What attracts the others in this meeting to run away from the complexity of the situation and issues?' To break the collective flight in the meeting the leader or individual group member could say, for instance, 'I can see that it is fun to fight and name the enemy, but I don't see how it helps us face the situation or get done what we need to do.'

'Be a hero, save us!'

In this scenario the group is in thrall to the leader. The group sinks into compliance mode and is unified by its hatred of an external enemy. In that sense it is similar to fight and flight, except it all feels much more intense, and disturbed. Anyone in the group not toeing the line is scapegoated, and certainty replaces curiosity and critical thinking.

The symptoms of this are that everyone thinks in the same way, uses similar buzzwords and admires the leader too much; group members are too frightened to speak their mind, while the leader can't get enough adulation and is attracted to being the 'lone hero'. Psychologically, such charisma-dependent groups are very hard to resist, and group members in such meetings tend to withdraw and feel helpless inside.

We have seen many people in the upper layers of management behave like this. We appreciate that it is hard to escape this pattern but also know that it is unhealthy. There are two options that are open to anyone who wants to escape helplessness and powerlessness, First, to wait until the group and leader are stuck and then make a contribution like: 'I feel stuck and I don't seem to be alone, perhaps we can step back and think what is going on and what would help us to take the next step?' Second, to try to identify the 'elephant in the room' and ask the leader (or someone you trust in the group) directly whether it would help to name the elephant before pressing on with the agenda.

Meetings serve a purpose – even if it's not the one it says on the tin

We were asked to review the strategy board of a large public body. The chair wanted to hear the views of members of the board and to check whether adjustments were needed to ensure the board met its purpose. We talked to most of the 25 members of the group and observed the board in action. It quickly became clear that the group was neither a 'board' nor that strategic. It did not take the key decisions – the three leaders at the top of the organization held tight control of these. Nor did the group focus on strategy. A lot of the group's time was spent exchanging information and updating each other on progress and changing circumstances.

However, what also emerged clearly was that the group was a much valued forum for senior people across the organization. Members of the group had the opportunity to meet three or four times a year. They heard from senior leadership about the latest developments in government and outside. Formally and informally, they developed a shared sense of the context within which they were working. A lot of the value of meetings was in the side conversations people had. One member said: 'I always come with a list of the six or seven people I need to talk to while I'm at the board.'

And the most powerful effect of the meetings was to develop a community of leaders across the organization. Individuals talked about meeting members of the group in other situations and feeling an immediate link and sense of identity with them. 'We know now that we are community leaders and have a shared sense of purpose.'

So what was the impact of the review? It did not lead to a radical change in the purpose of the board, or to a big shift in the way the group worked. What it did do was reconcile people to the value of the meetings and the role that they had. People stopped pretending to be the strategy group and were happy instead to be a 'Leaders' Forum'.

The value of meetings

From an anthropologist's point of view, meetings are a habit that can't be given up. A meeting can be seen as a ritual occasion with a quasi-religious purpose; it is the embodiment of the formal organization. There is a liturgy (agenda) with an opening ritual that includes apologies for absence and matters arising. It has agenda items and it has a 'holy text', the minutes. It also has a concluding rite where the date of the next meeting is fixed and any other business can be raised (often generating the need for another meeting). Usually meetings take place in a designated room and are led by a priest-like figure who dresses formally for the occasion to indicate status differential. In longer meetings participants will 'break bread' together in the form of finger food and biscuits. The function of this ceremony is to find a way to share a sense of common identity and purpose, avoiding the difficult issue of moving in and out of power and status differences. Sometimes longer strategy meetings are held offsite and an independent facilitator employed to conduct the relevant rituals.

You may not instinctively sympathize with the idea that meetings have a hidden religious meaning, but it does illustrate that when we meet there is an awful lot going on. What is 'on the table' (the agenda) at the meeting may be less important than what is 'off the table' and cannot be spoken about. In many respects every meeting is a manifestation of what is described in the other chapters of this book – strategy, leadership, management, change, power, politics, groups and community are all present and playing out. Even the most straightforward meeting involves huge complexity. The meeting itself is the tip of the iceberg of organizational life. In the face of this realization, it is tempting either to become a fundamentalist about task and procedure by holding strictly to the explicit task and agenda, or to give up because you cannot possibly know what's going on, so don't even try.

Work on and off the table

Making meetings work – what you can do

Choose which meetings you attend

Meetings are not a replacement for work, they *are* your work, and therefore need to be taken seriously by you. We think that most leaders participate in too many meetings, without sufficient breathing space. The first step in taking yourself, and your time, seriously is to make strategic and tactical choices about which meetings merit your attendance – and to leave space in the diary to allow for adequate preparation and follow-up. In deciding which meetings to attend, it is useful to think not only about the task of the meeting but also the group that makes up the meeting. What is your connection to that group? How significant are they to you now? This is not only a utilitarian calculation; it is also existential, as we described in Chapter 5.

In choosing which meetings to go to you are choosing which groups you want to be part of, a critical aspect of leadership. Getting things done through groups involves investment in the social relationships of the people involved. The meeting is the place and the time where work is co-ordinated, monitored, planned and distributed. It is also the place where an organization can re-enforce or adapt its existing culture in the light of external circumstances. The pattern of the meeting and the way the conversation ebbs and flows changes or recreates the local culture, as Isobel's story illustrates.

See every meeting as a three-act play

A good drama has us on the edge of our seats. Intellectually, we are gripped by the intricacy of the plot and the 'who done it?' Emotionally we are engaged by the heroes and villains we care about. To get things done together, it is important for the leader to work with relationships and emotions as well as with the task in hand. You can think of this as the unfolding drama of the group in the meeting. What happened in the previous episode? How can you model helpful group behaviour and challenge sabotaging acts of deviance that undermine joint efforts? It is not a matter of learning to manipulate the emotions in the room intelligently, but of treating emotions as real, accepting their importance to everyone and gathering the intelligence and data that the emotions in the meeting afford leader and participant. It is at the relationship and feeling level that leaders and group members can sense and understand

189

what is easy, what is difficult, what needs to be addressed, and what gets in the way of working together effectively.

To extend this metaphor, if you want your meetings to be more effective and productive, whether they are face-to-face or virtual, the 'three-act play' is a useful way to think about them.

Act 1. Preparation

Both group and leader need a feeling that it is their group or a cross-section of their organization that is meeting. To this end it is best if everyone knows why they are in the group, and what the purpose of the meeting is.

Ask yourself:

- What needs to be on the agenda and what can be taken off?

- How can others be involved in shaping the agenda?

- What is the exact purpose of each agenda item (to give/seek information; to solve a problem; to make a decision; to give or get opinions; to elicit ideas)?

- Who will lead each agenda item? Who will be responsible for follow-up?

- Who needs preparing and briefing before the meeting?

- If it's a virtual meeting, what internet or telephone technology is being used? Is it reliable? Do participants know how to use it? What training or information is needed before the meeting?

- What is a good order/flow for the items on the agenda? Starting with an 'easy' topic, having a heavy topic in the middle, and then pinning things down at the end works well.

We often observe those in authority trying to do too much on their own – work out the agenda, chair the discussion, hold people to account, ascertain what needs to be done, try to ensure everyone contributes, summarize discussions, draw out conclusions and identify next steps. Hold all the business issues and consider relationships and group dynamics. It's too much for any one person! We need to get help from others.

There is often a critical moment when the person in authority stops trying to do it all on their own and starts relying on the group. Often leaders use facilitators to manage *how* the group works – to ensure everyone has a voice, that the key questions are considered, that the group gets through the work needed – while they as leader focus on the *what* – the work the group needs to do.

We have talked about the tendency in most organizations to over-fill the agenda. A critical question is when, and how, the group makes time to step back from operational issues and stops to think together. It means keeping some space when there is no agenda, but time to reflect together on what is most important.

Act 2. The meeting itself

During a meeting:

Welcome – assert your authority and lead in a style that suits your personality.

Purpose, timings, order of meeting – make sure people know where the meeting is going and which agenda items are more important than others.

It is usually found helpful by a group if a meeting starts with a clear statement or exploration (depending on the formality or informality of the gathering) of the following key questions, related to building relationships *and* getting things done:

• What is the essential context for this meeting that everyone needs to be aware of?

- What is the work we need to do today?

- How do we want to go about it?

It's usually important to 'check in' with participants, so that everyone has the chance to find their voice and connect (enough) as people. We suggest going around the room and hearing from each person before the business begins:

- How are you? (Seek more of an answer than 'fine.') Then a more pointed and relevant question, such as 'What's on your mind today?'

We are constantly impressed by how much the quality of conversation improves if people have enough opportunity to connect with one another before (or as) they start the business discussion:

Signpost the agenda – make it clear why each item is on the agenda. Encourage discussion, exploration and decision making.

Invite others to lead agenda items they are responsible for.

Facilitate – remember to be in the service of the whole group. Notice the shifts in energy, in verbal and non-verbal communications. Notice your own emotions. Have a way of opening and closing down discussions and drawing out different standpoints. Confront resistance and name any 'elephants' – issues that are unspoken or being avoided.

If the meeting gets stuck, here are some useful prompts and questions:

- Try and say how you are feeling. It's often not easy, but it does help the group express emotions that block progress. Disclosure as a leader will encourage others to do the same.

- 'Right now I'm feeling proud/disappointed about we have achieved – how do others feel?'

192

- 'I sense there is something not quite right here – the unsaid is louder than the spoken – can someone articulate what the elephant in the room is that we are not discussing?'

- 'Let's separate the person from the issue.'

- Invite in those who are silent or quiet.

- 'You've said what you don't want to happen, Bill. Can you tell us what you would like to happen?'

- 'It seems to me that this conversation is going round in circles – let's have a proposal that we can work on . . .'

- Or, 'What is getting in the way for me is . . .'

Ending a meeting:

Ending a meeting needs to be done well because the beginning of the next meeting of the group will become attached to it. Finish on time and plan for the next meeting. Review questions could include:

- What next steps and actions are you taking away? (Hear from others what they going to do instead of recapping yourself.)

- How was this meeting for you (and what do we want to build on or do differently another time)?

- 'One thing I'm going to do differently as a result of this meeting is . . .' (Hear from each person.)

Act 3. Follow-up

There is a business part to this – ensuring that people are aware of commitments made and the actions that will follow; and a process part – ensuring adequate review and learning about how to work best as a group. Useful questions to ask yourself in relation to process include:

- Who had the most 'air time'?

- Who had the least 'air time'?

- How clear were the purposes of each task? Were people committed to them?

- How well did people listen to each other?

- Were creative ideas suggested?

- What happened to creative ideas?

- Did the group resolve or bury differences?

- Were difficult or unpleasant issues raised and resolved?

- How well was time used?

- Did the group deal in facts wherever possible?

- Did individual aims conflict?

- What actions helped the group most?

- What actions hindered the group?

Meetings are the place where all the issues discussed in this book – the settled enough self, groups and communities, strategy, power, politics, making a difference – play out. They provide the opportunity to experiment with different ways of working and influencing others, of influencing culture in the ways you consider important. Instead of being energy sapping and ineffective, meetings can be places where you discover how to be the leader you can be.

In Part 3 we look at the whole story of leading today. How can we break free of bonkers and make a difference?

PART 3

Breaking Free of Bonkers

CHAPTER 10

Breaking Free of Bonkers – A Test Case

Stories are central to this book. They illustrate and illuminate, but they also do much more than that. Storytelling is central to organizational life, and therefore to leading. Stories allow us to explore the complexity of organizations – power, politics, groups and communities – as they evolve and shift. By the stories we choose to tell, we send powerful messages about what is important and what is not.

We now want to tell a story (in which we were involved as organizational consultants) as an illustration of how you can work in a non-heroic way; how you can break free of bonkers.

The principal actors in this story are the National Institute for Health Research (NIHR) and R&D departments in the NHS. Our role was to consult with them in support of making NHS research faster and easier.

The story begins in a familiar way, with a written strategy and some metrics.

Life sciences and medical research were clear priorities in the Government's 2011 'Plan for Growth'. The objective was wealth creation and overcoming the split between public and private enterprise. The pharmaceutical industry and others told the government that research practice was mired in bureaucracy – it was too complicated and took too long for trials and studies to be approved, initiated and completed. The large global pharmaceutical companies, whose investment was critical, could look elsewhere. Research in the UK had to become faster and easier, and that meant that the R&D function in the NHS had to change.

For many people, the R&D departments were 'the problem'; the primary block to research becoming faster and easier. Over the years – in response to serious concerns about unethical and ungoverned research practice – an ever-increasing set of regulations and requirements for research practice had been created. The R&D departments in the NHS ensured that research met all the necessary requirements, but there was a bottleneck. This had to change, and so the government established benchmarks (or targets) for the time to set up, run and recruit to clinical trials.

Creating community – by invitation

In commissioning this work, the NIHR was in effect issuing an invitation to R&D leaders to be part of something with them. This was a significant move. Previously, the NIHR had 'stopped at the door' of NHS trusts on the basis that trusts were responsible for their own R&D function. The NIHR was crossing a significant boundary. Politics was also alive and well since, from the early days of the NIHR, the story had grown that it would 'do away with the need for R&D in trusts'. It didn't matter that this was never the intention.

So to invest in the development of the function in this way was an important move, but not without its complications and implications, as we shall see. Notice though how the idea of invitation can create interest, energy and excitement. Invitations carry with them a sense of possibility.

Working differently

In the heroic orthodoxy it is conventional for the consultants to follow the medical model; to investigate what's wrong through some tests, and based on the results to diagnose and prescribe a solution. Embedded in this way of thinking is the idea that the work, or the planned change, starts at the implementation phase, post-diagnosis.

There are two critical flaws with this. First, imagining that consultants can stand outside the situation and know more (or better) than those who are fully immersed in the organization. Consultants will often be called in on the basis that they can give an 'objective' view of the situation. We think not. We can only give *our* view of the situation; *our* understanding of the multiple stories that are being told about the situation, and the impact that this is having. Secondly, the assumption is that any work undertaken in the diagnostic phase is somehow neutral; that when a consultant, sent by the boss, turns up and has a conversation with you about your view of the organization, you are completely unaffected by it. We think not. The work starts the moment anyone is touched by the interaction. From that point the existing state of affairs is called into question; changing the conversation changes things.

For both of these reasons (and more) our first move was to listen to the stories of those working in and leading the R&D function. Over a period of weeks we spent a couple of hours, or at most half a day, in around 20 organizations, usually with the R&D director, senior manager and their teams. We also spoke to numerous medical researchers about their experience of the R&D function.

Unsurprisingly, we heard different stories. We met many dedicated R&D managers and directors who well understood the need for faster and easier research, and were as frustrated as the next person by the bureaucratic mire. However, we also found a fragmented world in which R&D leaders felt disconnected from those 'making the national rules' who, they felt, did so without listening to their experience and expertise. We found researchers frustrated by their experience of R&D, which could degenerate into shouting, in person or by email. We found R&D directors and managers with very different experiences of life and work – often operating quite separately from one another.

Getting connected

There were two of us doing this work, seeing people separately. We shared our notes as we went along and began to develop a short paper reflecting on these encounters and the implications for what we might offer. We shared this paper with people that we met and invited them to respond.

In this way we were developing our thinking about how we would approach this work, but more significantly, we were creating a relationship with this community. We were seeking to come alongside them in their situation. We encountered a world of experts, many of whom felt excluded, devalued and 'done unto'. We were working for the NIHR. The story about doing away with R&D had stuck in the minds of R&D leaders who were suspicious of us. We knew that whatever we did we had to do it *with* them and not *to* them. The experience of these early encounters, and the themes that emerged, posed some challenging questions about how to respond.

Filling up and freeing up – expert knowledge

The traditional joke about consultants is that they borrow your watch and then tell you the time. In other words, what does the consultant know? We were often asked the following question: 'What do you know about R&D in the NHS?'

In the highly regulated world of R&D, expertise counts for a lot, just as it does in many walks of life. In many situations there are requirements to be met and a right way to do things. There was a competence model for R&D leaders and it was suggested that we could use this as the basis for our approach. We were also contacted by a number of experts working in the field – providers of training who would also assess the competence of R&D departments and make recommendations for improvement. They offered to help us develop the content for the work.

We were doubtful. To us it seemed that we had entered a world that was full of advice – most of it written down in endless guidance and regulation. An approach of training people, based on an idealized competence model, would not work. We had met people who wanted to be freed up, not filled up with more advice and guidance – which most of them knew very well anyway. However, this made us anxious. We knew it was not our job to be R&D experts, but expertise had its place, and it seemed safer to include such expertise in our plans. We would not be criticized for doing that. And there's the rub – 'we would not be criticized'. To offer more expert content would be non-contentious to a world in which expert knowledge was the source of authority and standing in the community. If it didn't work it would not be our fault but that of the 'delegates'.

But we were not thinking of delegates, we were thinking of participants, and counting ourselves as participants. To label the people we had met as delegates creates an 'us and them' in which power lies mostly with 'us'. It is a pedagogical method that turns consultants into tutors or teachers. We realized that to include expert content would be a defence against our anxiety. We would be hiding behind expertise rather than addressing the situation.

As the work developed we realized that our job was to own our authority that 'we change the world one conversation at a time'. By being bold about this we set an example and encouraged our clients to own their authority.

Power and status differences

In our enquiry work we were struck by the significant differences between R&D directors and managers, particularly their professional career paths and personal history. Typically, R&D directors are men – medical doctors, researchers in their own right, part-time (sometimes a day a week or less) in the R&D director role with a portfolio of other clinical and non-clinical responsibilities. They are not members of the top executive management team, but usually report to the medical director. R&D directors will 'do the job for a few years because someone has to'. Their clinical academic colleagues are their peers. Often they find themselves as the first port of call for a disgruntled researcher complaining about the R&D office and 'what they have done now!'

Typically, R&D senior managers are women and in the role full time. They find themselves in a career in research management through a variety of routes. Sometimes it is through completing a PhD and post-doctoral research before research management. Others have a clinical background, often nursing, and for still others their career begins as a research administrator. After a few promotions they find themselves as the most senior manager, expert in the research process and the many requirements that must be met. For the manager this is a career; for the director this is one job among several, a staging post.

We came to think of this relationship as akin to 'upstairs, downstairs' in the English stately home – the directors 'upstairs' with their privileged colleagues, thinking great thoughts and doing great research; the managers 'downstairs' with their administrative colleagues, 'keeping the show on the road' so that those 'upstairs' were relatively untroubled by 'administration'. As the analogy suggests, there are significant differences in power and status. We came to use this analogy early on, right at the start of working with a group of managers and directors. It was always the one that sparked the most lively conversations – some seeing it as 'hitting the nail on the head', others protesting 'it's not like that where we work'. Perhaps there was a culture clash between (included) directors who largely accepted power differences and (excluded) managers who wanted to be a on a level and involved in decision making.

However, for them to have the 'upstairs, downstairs' conversation managers and directors had to be in the room together. Our client had expected that we would work with managers as part of a process focused on individual leadership development, confirming 'downstairs' as the problem. How many times have you heard that? We were sure that it was the *relationship* between manager and director that was central. So much that is characteristic of R&D and the potential to make research 'faster and easier' is caught up in that relationship. At the extremes the manager is the servant of the researchers – it is their job to 'deal with the administration and make it right'. Power lies with the director, who may see their job as being to represent the interests of researchers, and to ensure that R&D doesn't 'make life difficult' for researchers, as if researchers themselves have no responsibility.

This relationship is at the heart of the shift that the NIHR was seeking to lead. Before the NIHR was created research was concentrated in fewer centres, funding was based on previous history and research was seen a separate activity for elite clinicians who had university (as opposed to NHS) contracts. The bold move that the NIHR made in its early days was to take the money and allocate it based on clear criteria and contracts. This process is continuing, and now research is a multifaceted partnership between patients, public, the NHS, universities, pharmaceutical and other medical industries, all within an appropriate legal and ethical governance framework. In theory and in practice (sometimes), all the partners benefit from this partnership so that health is improved and wealth is created in the process. However, like many complex partnerships, these relationships are often fraught with conflict and suspicion. Different institutions, for example an NHS trust and its partner university, have different goals, incentives and performance regimes to meet. In other words, it is easy for the partnership to split apart, and holding it together requires effort and an appreciation that power sometimes shifts between 'upstairs' and 'downstairs'.

This is the central work of the director and manager; to hold the relationships, with their inherent tensions, and not allow things to fall apart. They must hold together if the complex web of partnerships is to hold together. The obvious conclusion was that we should work with the director–manager partnership, and my colleague and I discussed this at length. We had met with some directors and found them ambivalent about working with us. We had met more managers and found them enthusiastic. For many managers the central issue was 'time with my director, I never see them!' We played with various ways of including the directors. In the end, we made it a requirement that organizations could only participate in the process if the director and manager joined as a pair. By doing so we insisted that these two people, who embodied the different cultures, worked together and avoided the madness of seeing each other as enemies. We opened a space in which they could discover more productive ways of working together.

The answer is questions

In the orthodox world, consulting is usually based on knowing the answer and selling certainty to the top team. It is then a matter of getting them – the group or groups who are 'the problem' – to do it. We, on the other hand, did not have a blueprint, or even a vision for R&D. What we 'knew' was that there were many people leading, trying to make a difference, in isolation from each other, even in isolation from their leadership colleagues in the case of some pairs. We knew that an 'upstairs–downstairs' relationship was at best outdated, and that models of 'best practice' seemed abstract and irrelevant in the hurly-burly of daily life. We experienced the anxiety of working with benchmarks and the shame of public failure, and we knew that if we made the benchmarks the most significant measure we would be colluding with avoiding the critical work on relationships.

Eventually we formulated our design around three simple questions, each the focus of a workshop, each workshop separated by several months:

• What's going on in my context and what is my part in it?

• How do we raise our game?

• What have we got to say and to whom?

In between the first two workshops, the director and manager formulated their 'Improvement Intention' – the focus of their joint leadership – and separately asked around a dozen of their colleagues to respond to a qualitative 360 feedback. We then spent a day at each trust considering results of the 360s, and the Improvement Intention. We also encouraged the pair to talk with each other about what had emerged from their respective 360s and their pattern of working together.

Subsequently, managers work in 'Leading Improvement Groups', meeting for five separate days spread over 15–18 months. Each meeting is hosted by one of the trusts. The morning is spent understanding how R&D works at the site and the afternoon in 'Action Learning'.

At the third workshop the group creates a conference about what they want to say, now, on subjects of immediate relevance and concern. They invite the relevant guests and all other participating R&D leaders. In other words, it is an exercise in collective leadership which requires the group to take up their authority, for themselves and on behalf of the wider community.

Everything's connected

In orthodox leadership development the focus is on individual behaviour, often defined by a competence framework. To us this makes no sense. By definition, none of us leads alone. In leadership it is not what I do, or what you do; what matters most is *what we do between us and how we work together*. In the same way it is common to separate individual leadership development and organization development. This too seems to us a false separation. As we have seen, settling yourself requires you to consider what you are part of. In this work, manager and director are part of a pair, part of an R&D function and part of an NHS trust; and they are part of leading improvement and faster and easier research. As we worked with successive groups it became apparent that being part of a national community of R&D leadership was also critical.

Being in the middle

We encourage leaders, however senior, to see themselves as 'in the middle' in multiple ways. As we concluded the first phase of our work we found ourselves in a tricky 'middle' situation with our client. We were pressed to tell them what we had found in individual trusts. This was something we were not prepared to do. We had agreed with the trusts that individual situations would not be reported. Our client accepted this but pressed for a summary of what we had found.

In the orthodox consulting world there is usually considerable investment in the report at the end of the 'diagnostic' phase. It 'sums up' and brings clarity and certainty – 'this is the way that the world is', as if there were one truth about the situation. In our practice we are reluctant to put pen to paper in this way because it positions us as standing outside the situation, seeing objectively – which in our view is impossible. Furthermore, we had some challenging things to say about the situation, including the ways in which the NIHR had contributed to creating some of the very things they were complaining about. We thought carefully about what to write, worked and reworked what we said; sending it off felt risky. On the one hand it felt like it could jeopardize the work, and on the other hand it felt like, if we couldn't say these things, we would be dishonest and wasting our time and our client's money.

We argue that leadership is created *between us* and that what happens in organizations emerges in the chemistry and complexity of multiple relationships. Of course, this applies to the client–consultant relationship too, and so we have to confront the fundamental paradox in the orthodox view, a paradox that, from our perspective, is at the centre of consulting.

Leaders usually turn to consultants when they are anxious and they want to buy certainty – do X and Y will follow. And yet we are selling *uncertainty*, or at least the acceptance that the future is not knowable or predictable, and no amount of analysis or PowerPoint will make it so. To us uncertainty is normal, to be expected, in everyday life. It is not just anxiety provoking; it also creates energy and opens a space for new thoughts, conversations and actions.

By contrast, if the search is for certainty in a consulting assignment, client and consultant will often co-operate (or collude) in the creation of a singular view of the world – as it is now, and as it needs to become. This is a further example of idealization in the heroic orthodoxy, of the magical thinking that comes with it, resulting in the creation of false hope. We think 'we see the world as we are, not as it is'. Each of us has a different experience and in the groups that we belong to we often seek to reinforce our experience with that of others by telling each other stories that explain why the world is the way it is.

In this example we can see that the powerful pharmaceutical industry, which had the ear of government, was firmly of the view that R&D was the problem, and government had been persuaded. We saw this as an over-simplification, but we recognized that it was held as truth by many people. We did not want to enter into an argument about *the* truth; rather to bring into focus the multiple, different experiences and truths that those caught up in this world held to be the case. Just as some saw R&D as the problem, so some R&D leaders saw the NIHR as the problem. For some R&D leaders this meant they saw themselves as a victim of the powerful people making the impossible rules. All of this is an over-simplification of course, but it has a determining effect. If I tell myself I am a powerless victim of the bosses, or if I tell myself I am a powerless boss because of 'them', either way I free myself of any responsibility to do anything about the situation in which I find myself. Not least because I close down the space for an honest exchange of view and encourage mutual distrust.

A world-changing conversation

We were in a Whitehall meeting with the NIHR's senior team, including the national director, who was impressive, powerful and chairing the meeting. In the middle of the discussion about the R&D work the Director said (not for the first time): 'R&D departments are the problem here.' Quickly, one of her team, who is our client on a day-to-day basis, said 'you have got to stop saying that, we can't do this without them.' There was a pregnant pause. It proved to be a transformational moment from which there was no going back. A habitual pattern, or way of seeing the situation, had been named and brought into the light. As a result the pattern was broken. It had become impossible to say 'R&D is the problem' without challenge. A new, 'we are in this together' pattern had come to life. As with anything newly born, this new pattern would need nurturing by client, consultant and others. We have to act as if we are on the same side, even if it doesn't always feel like that.

To enter into a consulting contract is to make a *joint* commitment, a partnership between client and consultant. There is risk on both sides. Our fortunes are tied together, and like it or not, we are dependent on one another. Just as in any relationship, the mutual dependence can be joyful and rewarding but can also descend into mutual recrimination and resentment. There are anxious times for consultant and client. However, as long as there is commitment to each other and the overall task, client and consultant can remain curious about the situation, challenge each other in seeking fresh insights, and experiment with what can be changed by acting together. By doing this we begin to understand how each of us sees the situation we are trying to address, what each of us might contribute, and what we need each other for.

Critically, this also requires us to explore our limits and what we *cannot* offer to one another. Sometimes the client wants the consultant to be a superhero, and it can be tempting to play to this fantasy. Hence the need to strive for a 50:50 relationship through an adult conversation about respective needs and whether or not they can be met. This 50:50 test can also be applied to the many unspoken 'contracts' we make with each other on a daily basis at work.

Power and politics – creating group boundaries

This moment of shared commitment in Whitehall felt like a breakthrough. However, for R&D leaders nothing had changed. They knew that they were perceived as 'the problem' and we were working in an environment in which performance against benchmarks would be made public. R&D leaders knew that, beyond those quantifiable measures, their performance was discussed by the NIHR.

We were asking the group to undertake some intimate work, on themselves and as a pair, to examine how their relationship was working. How much of this would be shared, and with whom? There was suspicion, and we were challenged by the group to say whom we were working for. Through this conversation we came to the formulation that the NIHR were our commissioners and the group our clients. This allowed us to negotiate some boundaries about what was regarded as public and shared with the group and the NIHR and what was private or held within the group. Together we learnt the importance of negotiating these boundaries to build up trust and belief in each other.

For a group that was used to being 'done unto' this was critical. We learnt later that in the early days there had been an expectation that 'nothing will happen' as a result of our work because that was the previous pattern. This was fuelled by the length of time that it took to start work with a group. We came to realize that we were working with a group who saw themselves as outsiders, bypassed by the development of the NIHR, with low expectations that anything would change. With hindsight we can see that the shift that the group prompted us to make – that we were working for *them* – was critical.

In the heroic world of orthodox consulting, the primary objective is to think your way through a problematic situation on behalf of top management. Typically, the consultant's work is owned by the most senior figure; consultant and client share the same definition of 'the problem' and progress towards the solution, which can and should be measured. Often we are hired because we have a different view of organizations and leadership, typically one that is not fully shared with our clients. This can be useful because working with difference brings with it the possibility of change, and it is also pragmatic. If we had to ensure that client and consultant held a thoroughly consistent theoretical base, most of the work would not get off the ground. So, sitting with the client and holding a different perspective is part of the work, and it produces its own anxiety; deciding when and how to offer that different perspective, feeling compromised sometimes by keeping quiet when all sorts of untested assumptions are being aired, is all part of the task.

We sat between the NIHR and the R&D leaders. They saw the world differently and we knew that it was important to hold a strong relationship with both (and other key players too), to hold ourselves in the middle.

For example, in the orthodox view of organizations it is usually assumed that people have singular reporting lines and loyalties. However, as we saw in Chapter 6, most people, even if they have a single boss, also have multiple loyalties to hold and negotiate. In this story the significance of the NIHR and its funding varied significantly from organization to organization. Some trusts were almost entirely dependent on their NIHR income, others much less so. The level of dependency has a significant impact on the relationship because power is mediated through need to a significant extent. If I need you more than you need me, you are more powerful that I am. For an organization or individual researcher, developing a resilient research portfolio means holding multiple relationships with commercial, government and charitable funders; not putting 'all your eggs in one basket'. For us to stand alongside R&D leaders we had to recognize and name these conflicting loyalties, for them and for ourselves. Encouraging this (usually) unspoken reality of conflicting loyalties to be discussed allows boundaries to be openly negotiated and conflicts to be held and contained. For those involved in the work, this was a new way of working with change and development.

We also tried to hold a middle position in relation to the benchmarks for R&D performance. The primary reason for our commission was to make research 'faster and easier', and if we were to attach ourselves too closely to the benchmarks we would not be credible. Benchmarks, or targets, are a blunt instrument in a complex world. Holding a position that benchmarks are part (and only *part*) of the work created some anxiety for us. What if trusts chose not to pay any attention to the benchmarks? What if the numbers got worse? We spoke openly with the group about the need for 'faster and easier' research, and our perspective on performance targets. We spoke openly about the different perspectives and interests. This enabled people to work on the real issues and reach workable solutions.

Power and politics – inter-group rivalry

There were various persistent tensions between the CRN (the Clinical Research Network arm of the NIHR) and the R&D directors and managers about who does what and how they hold each other to account. The CRN allocates a significant amount of money to trusts, and this has a direct bearing on trust staffing and capacity. Some R&D directors and managers feared that the CRN wanted to take over their role. This tricky relationship became more vexed during a national reorganization of the CRN, which rationalized multiple networks into 15 regions. As a consulting team we heard many stories of fraught relationships, and we became increasingly concerned. In private, we – the consulting team – talked about the nature of our responsibility. We had no mandate to work with the CRN, yet it was obvious that the CRN and R&D were in this together, and their fate was deeply interconnected. We felt we would be washing our hands of something of which we were a part if we did nothing. So we used our influence with the NIHR to convene an additional national meeting between the trusts we were working with and the CRN.

The meeting evolved into a large gathering with the national and local leaders of all the research networks, other key players including the NIHR, and most of the 64 trusts we were working with at the time. For many of the R&D leaders this was a cathartic meeting and a chance to express themselves and their concerns. For some of the CRN leaders it was traumatic; they felt outnumbered and on the spot. There were some painful exchanges. The meeting continues to live on in the collective organizational memory and is still talked about; for some as an achievement, for others as a 'never again' experience. There are stories about things having changed for the better as a result, and stories of nothing changing.

Making a difference – changing the story

Since we began our consulting work with this client, medical research in England has become 'faster and easier'. Many of the trusts that we worked with significantly improved their performance, as did other trusts that were not part of the group. Of course, as is always the case, there were many other local and national changes occurring in parallel with our work. It would be convenient to attach a proportion of this achievement to our work in a linear 'cause and effect' way, but that would offend our understanding of how organizations work and how change happens. Just as importantly, the story has changed – not only the story that is told about R&D in general but also the story that R&D leaders tell themselves about their situation and their power.

For example, there was a moment early on when one of the R&D directors rehearsed the conventional wisdom that 'R&D will never be the priority for an NHS trust'. He went on to explain that he therefore had relatively little power and influence. This was a wonderful illustration of how 'the story I tell myself about myself' profoundly affects how you act, and so we challenged him in the group. It was early days and it felt risky. The following day began with the group reflecting on the previous day, and the robustness of this exchange stood out for some. It established a pattern of directness that persisted for us, a group of consultants, and for the R&D leaders. This particular director and manager pair went on to persuade their board to invest an additional £3 million in R&D over three years. Accepting that your work is not *the* priority also requires you to take responsibility for finding out where your work does sit in the multiple priorities of a large and complex organization.

Storytelling is powerful because it is human, social and brings connection and meaning to our lives. We tell each other stories and we do this repeatedly so that we perfect the stories as time goes on. The story used to be that R&D leaders had become disconnected and isolated from each other, and that the NIHR had arrived 'to do away with R&D in NHS trusts'. The story was one of exclusion, powerlessness and being 'done unto'. Within the trusts R&D managers represented the police force that stopped researchers doing what they wanted to do.

Individual R&D leaders, director–manager pairs and the connected community of R&D leaders now share, and retell, a different story. Research creates better care not only through findings but also by creating curiosity in the care process. R&D keeps research and the NHS trust safe; it is a key part of the NHS that treats, teaches and researches. It is a vital part of a world-leading industry and a critical area for economic growth.

The group has been discovering what it means for R&D to 'be itself' and be part of something. There is a different story to be told.

Changing the world one conversation at a time

While this story is written from the consultant's perspective, it is also a story about leadership, change and strategy, and how they work in practice. We offer our guiding principles here because they may be useful to you in your world:

- **Relationship comes before task and leadership before management** – disconnected people do disconnected work and put the managerial cart before the leadership horse. We retained our primary focus on leadership.

- **If you really want to change, focus on 'what is'** – talking about 'shoulds' takes us away from examining our current experience. We realized that our job was to describe our current experience of them and their world in order to encourage them to do the same with each other. That way we deepen our connection and commitment to each other and the world cannot stay as it is.

- **Local matters most** – we realized it was our job to hold R&D leaders' 'feet to the fire' of taking local action first and foremost, not giving away their power to national organizations and others.

- **We 'change the world one conversation at a time'** – Peter Block's phrase that we came to see as the 'red thread' running through the work. We didn't think about it in this way at the time, but it was why we configured the work for R&D managers and directors in the way we did. We could come alongside them, and if they could change their conversation then there was always a good chance they could begin to change the world.

Conversations add up

We learnt together as we worked with the R&D community. We made sense together. We worked with the grain of their organizations and cultures. We offered what we knew; we did not set ourselves apart but learnt with them.

In the next chapter we extend this approach to change and development to what you can do as a leader. In a bonkers world, with a dominant heroic orthodoxy, how can individuals make a difference? How can you break free of bonkers and help the people and organizations around you learn and adapt to changing circumstances?

CHAPTER 11

Making a Difference in a Bonkers World

'Never doubt that a small group of thoughtful, committed citizens can change the world; indeed, it's the only thing that ever has.'

Margaret Mead, *Sex and Temperament*

Despair, giving up, is ever-present. In the face of a world where management and leadership are turned upside down, where there is an addiction to change, and strategy belongs more to the realm of fantasy than reality, small wonder we ask ourselves 'What difference can I make?' The world that we aspire to live in, the ambition that we hold for our organization, can seem an impossibility. Sometimes it seems that our only option is to wish the orthodoxy away, naïvely, or to become cynical.

In this book we seek to be hopeful and realistic. Writer and blogger Maria Popova writes that 'critical thinking without hope is cynicism, but hope without critical thinking is naivety'. This is what we have been exploring. For example, we can be cynical about organizational politics and the endless round of meetings that fill our diaries. Or we can be hopeful that what we do matters, at least to some extent, and dedicate ourselves to the art of the possible.

In this chapter we tackle the question: 'So how do I make a difference?'

Leading as a craft

We think that leadership is best understood as a craft, not as a science or a profession. It is a craft that we learn by being apprentice to leaders that we admire, and others who perhaps we despise. Either way, we gather ideas about the kind of leader we do or do not want to become. As we describe in the chapter on the settled self, it starts with each of us. 'I am not clarifying what I think, feel and intend so that I can impose my will on you. I am doing that work so that I can be as clear as possible in my advocacy and then step back from it. This allows you the space to enquire into your experience, and to respond, so that I can listen to your advocacy. In order to take your experience seriously I have to be prepared to take my own experience seriously. This is why the cycle of preparation, engagement and reflection is so important.'

Just like the apprentice, we learn from our day-to-day experience of doing the work of a leader. As we become more experienced and skilled, we become a journeyman or woman who knows enough about the craft of leadership to be able to lead on a wider canvas and between narrow interests. We don't learn to develop our craft alone, we learn with and through groups and communities. We hold onto our professional roots as an engineer, electrician, teacher, nurse, accountant or whatever specialism we were first part of. That remains an important part of our identity, but along the way we discover other 'parts' that have meaning for us and within which we aspire to lead. Just like the master, our leadership craft is not something that is separate from us. It is part of who you are and is unique to you. There are ways in which your leadership may resemble that of others, just as an artist may be identified with a particular school, but your leadership will always be peculiarly yours. When the cracks open up in the heroic orthodoxy, as they did for many of the leaders whose story we tell, how you respond and lead will be down to you and the groups that you are part of.

If we are to develop leading as a craft, we need to take our experience seriously, value it and reflect on it, with others. We know a great deal that is tacit. We cannot name 'it'; indeed, we are not quite sure what 'it' is, except that it can be an effective guide in the moment. We are able to act, intuitively or unconsciously, in ways that work. Part of the work of leading is to slow down, to reflect from time to time, and become more aware of what 'it' is – so that we can see how to learn and adapt as circumstances change.

Leading involves being inspired, dedicated and hands-on

Just as the master sculptor is confident about an image, and curious about what will emerge when working with a new block of marble, so it is with our leadership. As leaders our 'marble' is the conversational life of the groups of which we are part. If I believe that we can change the world one conversation at a time, then I will pay exquisite attention to our meeting and my part in it. I don't think of myself as a passenger or observer. What I do, don't do or say matters – to you and to me – and may therefore make a difference.

Changing the conversation can feel demanding in part because by doing so we are implicitly changing the way power is distributed and used between us. Furthermore, this requires us to change the story that we tell ourselves about the situation we are in. As previously described, if we stick with the same 'nothing changes' conversation, chances are we will talk about what other people (not in the room) have done to make our lives impossible. Therefore, we are powerless and it is not our fault. This is a convenient truth because it allows you to believe that since you have no power you have no responsibility to do anything. What you do won't make a difference so why bother? You give up.

The power of believing that we change the world one conversation at a time is that it never lets us off the hook; nor do we feel overwhelmed by the task. We are continuously confronted with the choice of speaking, not speaking, saying the same thing, saying something different. I have to accept the consequences of going along with the prevailing pattern or not. I have nothing to complain about. It's up to me to make a difference.

To some this simple idea that our leadership craft depends on our ability to change the conversation will seem too small. Leadership is about big things like vision, grand designs and direction. We think not. Those that make a difference, and even achieve great things, do so because they pay attention to things as they are and take small, conversational, steps. They remain curious about the world; what's there, not there and why that might be. They refuse to reduce life to the rational, selfish consumer that the neo-liberal economist would have us become. They see a world that is also full of kindness and generosity, and in which we choose to work together for things that matter. Even when they are overwhelmed by doubts they find it in themselves to say 'enough, for now'.

Being in the middle

What we see is that successful leaders accept, and position themselves to be, *in the middle* of things. This is very different from imagining yourself to be above and apart from your organization. We are in the middle in many different ways.

Of past, present and future

We are in the middle *temporally*. Past, present and future, how we understand them and what we expect from them, are all with us, now. All have an influence on how we are and how we view things.

As we have seen, denigrating the past and the present is central to orthodox belief; it justifies riding roughshod over well-established communities of knowledge and practice. It is as if leaders are expected to encourage amnesia, but 'memory produces hope in the same way that amnesia produces despair' as theologian Walter Brueggemann observed. We suggest understanding the past in all its complexity, not as a romantic golden age; and we suggest seeing the present as dynamic and shifting, not fixed and immutable. Because, as the writer Rebecca Solnit notes, 'when you don't know how much things have changed, you don't see that they are changing or that they can change'.

If we want to make a difference, we need to be able to see the origins of the circumstances in which we find ourselves, and how things are already changing. Things may be changing for the better or for the worse, but nothing comes from nothing, and nothing stands still.

Socially

We are in the middle *socially*. We cannot lead alone and we can only discover what it means to be ourselves by being part of something. The groups that we identify with are always with us, even when we are alone. We are likely to be part of and identify with

223

multiple groups which will at times lead to conflicting loyalties and the sense that we have to choose between groups with which we may identify equally. Of course, we can only choose for ourselves, not for others, and allow that our choice may influence theirs. This matters because we can only make a difference by working with and through others, by relying on the group to enhance our leadership and connect well with groups and into communities.

To engage in serious development with others, you need to connect with them as people and not labels. How do you do this? You listen; you take an intelligent interest in the other person's needs and perspectives. You show that you are interested in their reality and that you appreciate their contribution. You don't assume things or project your feelings or views onto the other person. You accept the other person for who they are. You hear them. You show respect and demonstrate trust in their expertise and know-how.

We have repeatedly seen that people will not take the initiative, will not be able to gather their wits, unless they connect with others and feel heard and valued. That's your first job with other people. How often have you met leaders who are in 'transmit mode' and don't seem interested in what you are doing? How then do the people we relate to experience us? Do we listen and hear what they are saying? Do we take their experience seriously? Are we responsive to their concerns?

Positionally

We are in the middle *positionally*. We may have a job title that sounds like we are at the top of the organization, but that can be a trap. Whatever our position, we will find ourselves being squeezed (or maybe pulled apart) by legitimate, competing demands and pressures. The chair of a board is in the middle of the demands of financial backers for a return on their investment and the need to create an executive team that can lead a sustainable organization. The head of department is in the middle of delivering targets and projects demanded by their bosses and is also trying to do what they think is needed.

What we notice is that, far from seeing themselves as God, many of the most effective leaders we work with are modest. They speak about 'we' not 'I', and focus on groups and institutions and the work they do, not the individuals who lead. They understand that the collective dynamic and intention matters more than the individual leader. They notice that they are creating something together, something which is 'ours', not 'mine' or 'yours'.

Often, creating powerful alliances does not happen through formal projects and programmes, but conversation by conversation. We see senior leaders who want to tackle contentious, complex issues involving powerful groups, meeting others on their ground or neutral territory to signal that they are peers seeking to find a way through together. As has been pointed out by Nicholas Timmins, 'You can achieve almost anything, so long as you don't want to take the credit for it.' You have to 'give away ownership.'

We see leaders who act beyond, or outside, the limits of their formal, positional authority. No one told them to take responsibility and to champion a specific cause or development. They reached out, beyond their own groups, professions and formal responsibilities to build effective alliances with people in different fields. In doing so they were part of creating groups with sufficient shared values, principles or goals to act with a common purpose and make a difference. They allowed their leadership to be shaped by the group so that their leading was experienced as a shared endeavour and not as manipulation.

Ideologically

We are in the middle *ideologically*. A fundamental premise of this book is that neo-liberal economics, supported by the positivistic understanding of organizations and leadership, is an inadequate

Join up people and groups

way of understanding people and organizations. However, many of our clients remain strongly attached to this way of thinking, and that is likely to be true of your organization as well. It is a voice that you hear in the groups of which you are part. We are not suggesting that you seek to eliminate this voice in order to replace it with your own ideology or paradigm. We are suggesting that the work of a leader is to recognize and work with multiple ideologies and belief systems that will inevitably be present in the groups and communities that you work with. Just as we advocate pluralism in society as a whole, so we need to value it within and across organizations. Making a difference is less about right and wrong, and more about finding practical ways through complex and challenging circumstances.

Personally

We are in the middle *personally*. To be human is to live in a constant state of becoming. It is said that 'Life can only be understood backwards; but it must be lived forwards'. We see this most obviously in our children's early years but it is only later in life that we discover what it means to be in the middle of life and death.

At work, more prosaically, we are always in the middle of our *careers* – reflecting on what we have achieved, on what we have ambition for, and the price we are willing to pay for it. Later on we are in the middle of employment and retirement, and what those things might mean. Of course, positioning employment and retirement in that way makes it appear to be a straightforward binary choice, just as the phrase 'work–life balance' creates a false dichotomy. Work is part of life and vice versa. I am always in the middle of work and life, they are not alternatives, but I cannot know one without knowing the other. Underneath the desire to shape or change the organizational landscape are very personal issues like proving your parents wrong, setting a better example to the employees than the boss you had yourself, or the drive to assuage a number of deep-seated anxieties such as self-doubt, fear of failure or overcoming a sense of inadequacy.

Emotionally and rationally

We are in the middle of how we *think and feel*. As we have seen, the orthodox view of leadership and organizations limits us to our thoughts and reasoning, to quantifiable results and outcomes. In other words, we are required to restrict discussion to so-called 'objective' reality. As we explored in Chapter 2, the 'facts, figures and measures' that we call 'objective' are abstracted approximations that tell only a small part of the story. How much something costs tells us little about how much we value it. Leading groups and organizations requires us to draw on all of ourselves, our inner emotional experience and the resources of the group. 'The facts' are only ever one dimension. When we make a choice we make it with our head and our heart.

For many leaders this takes them into uncomfortable, personal territory. Talking about 'how I feel' is embarrassing. Typically, if emotions are running high we call a halt to proceedings. Perhaps we don't want to upset anyone or we fear we will fall out, or fall apart, so 'let's keep our feelings out of it'. By doing so, we create a perfect trap for ourselves.

The temptation to shut off feelings is strong. Feelings can seem like a threat to the rational, objective, intelligent selves that leaders pride themselves on being. Inevitably, these feelings usually surface in the end, and often in ways that are counter-productive. Our experience is that the most successful leaders have a different approach. They are prepared to get in touch with their feelings and to explore what they may tell them about themselves and about the situation they are in. With some trusted others, they seek to make sense of what's happening. They are then much better able to deal with circumstances and identify what the art of the possible may be in their situation.

Study after study has shown that the most resourceful work groups are capable of tolerating the strong feelings that come with serious disagreements and arguments, without falling apart. They are able to stay with the discomfort and pain of disagreeing without running away or becoming hysterical. They are loyal to each other and trust that things can be resolved. They will debate and disagree long enough to find a novel and creative way forward.

Both leaders and the people who work for them need to feel emotionally safe and attached enough, in order to lower their defences and share both their fears and their passions for change and creativity. Both change and innovation can be intellectually exciting and desirable while being emotionally frightening and unsettling. By modelling how to reveal the inner self and how to cope with being vulnerable, a leader gains acceptance and authority from the work group, opening up a space in which everyone's capacity for adaptation and innovation can safely surface.

Of the world as it is, and as it could be

Finally, and critically when it comes to leadership, we are in the middle of the *world as it is, and the world as it could be*. It is in this unsettling dissonance that we find the fuel and energy to make a difference. The tension between what is and what could be may frustrate us at times, but if we allow our impatience to get the better of us then our feet leave the ground and we take flight into abstract, idealized 'shoulds', losing the connection with our colleagues and the past and the present. It is perhaps intellectually stimulating to construct a picture of an idealized, imagined future, but it is just as likely to become a way of avoiding what's going on here and now. Andrew's story later in this chapter illustrates how effective leaders look and see for themselves; questioning, challenging and endorsing what they find, and in so doing, nurturing the future they aspire to create in the moment.

Recovering our senses – gaining some perspective

What are the implications for action if we see ourselves as *in the middle* of things?

If we accept that we are *in the middle*, in between, in many different ways, we see that there is no recipe, no one way to make a difference. How we lead is shaped by the context (the history and culture) we are in, the people and relationships we work with, the needs of each situation and what we are trying to achieve. Orthodox thinking tends to treat everything as a project with a definable beginning, middle and end. If we recognize the sheer complexity of being in the middle, then the limitations of this linear thinking become apparent. Using the discipline of project management (so long as it is subordinate to effective leadership) is useful in making a difference when we can be relatively clear and concrete about what we are trying to achieve. It is not enough when we are trying to be creative.

We need all our senses to do this well. This is both the burden and the joy for those who want to make a difference. The simple formulas don't work – and we have the capacity to make a difference, if we want to. We need to take our own experience seriously. We always need to be willing to learn. Every situation is slightly different. We need to experience what it is like to be in the middle of things, and we need to step back from time to time, as academic and author Ronnie Heifetz points out, to try and make sense of what is going on. Sometimes we need to take 'the balloon view'.

Look for the broader view

This means staying curious as a leader, asking simple direct questions that get to the heart of things; questions such as: 'How do things work at the moment?' 'When are you at your best?' 'What are the main problems?' 'What are we trying to achieve?' 'What is most important?' 'What are we learning?' 'What can we do?' 'What is the work that we need to do together?'

These questions draw others in and invite them to stay curious, to enquire into what makes an organization special. It involves considering the skills, qualities and experience that in one moment may be a great strength, and in another a weakness. It involves naming and facing difficulties and problems. It is the holding together of light and dark.

The temptation to retreat into simplistic management is strong. Often in the middle of a fraught meeting, which everyone wants to end, someone will say: 'We haven't got time for this, let's not reinvent the wheel. Others have already done this in X, Y or Z; let's copy what they did.' This usually prompts relief, followed quickly by agreement. In that moment, we have lost sight of our uniqueness. It is as if attending to what we are in the middle of and why we might be different from X, Y or Z is too much to bear. It is easier to wish away our difference, which is the essence of our humanity, and pretend we are all the same.

Even if you can establish that something is generally true, you cannot argue that it will be the case in any particular situation. This is why management and leadership recipes advocating a number of steps to being an effective leader (usually between three and seven) and leadership competence frameworks are of such limited value. Their fundamental mistake is that they rely on arguing, uncritically, from the general to the particular.

People need time and space to come together and bring to the surface the distinctive characteristics of their context, culture and history; the current business situation; the nature of the particular individuals and teams that you are working with. You are leading in the middle of an invisible cultural web. The groups, or group, that you are working with, large or small, have embedded habits and patterns of working together – 'It's the way things get done around here'. As touched upon in Chapter 6, the idea that you can take 'best practice' from elsewhere and 'plug and play' it in your own organization completely ignores this reality. Burke reminds us that there is wisdom held by institutions and groups that is the product of long experience, but which no one person can readily articulate. It is in reflecting, together, on practice that the wisdom becomes clearer.

Finding 'wiggle room'

What is needed are spaces for new ideas to be nurtured and for innovations to be developed. Sometimes that means dedicated teams, determined to succeed, trying lots of bold experiments in a short time; letting go quickly of approaches that don't show promise; working from the experience of previous developments, tacit and unconscious as well as explicit. A determination to press forward pragmatically until the result needed is achieved. It's what's happened in history again and again – the Manhattan Project; the development of the motor car; taking penicillin from the lab to a product that saved millions of lives; or indeed the Honda managers described in Chapter 4. Organizations and cultures adapted, new practices and thinking developed, great purposes were achieved. No one person could see or lead it all but some patterns are clear.

In an era in which the heroic orthodoxy seeks to fill every crevice of organizational life, finding such protected space is not easy. When we talk to successful leaders we are struck that many of them say, somewhat shamefacedly, that they 'worked under the radar' for a long time. In other words, they worked without formal permission or mandate; they kept planning, measurement and control mechanisms at arms' length; they kept out of the spotlight, away from detailed scrutiny and deadening processes for long enough. This is what we mean by 'wiggle room'.

Make spaces for experimentation

Modern organizations have systematically cleared away the spaces that used to exist in which controversy, exploration and renewal could happen. Like destroying the rainforest, they do so in the name of progress (cost reduction, efficiency, rooting out 'waste', alignment, transparency, good governance, control), but the effect is to obliterate areas where development can take place and on which the world depends for its survival. This process of regulating people's work lives is not new. It has been happening since industrialization, and before. It used to be cotton mills and car factories where employees were just 'hands' and every minute of the day was carefully controlled to ensure that no time was wasted. Now it is call centres and supply chain centres which are emblematic of the modern work disciplines.

Increasingly, to their horror, professionals have been caught up in the new ways of working, ways which are often driven by a need to fit people around the systems and the software, rather than the other way around. Teachers, doctors, nurses, psychiatrists, social workers, financial advisers – all are caught in a world of 'best practice' and protocols that leave less and less room for deviation from the prescribed way of working. Of course, these guidelines and protocols are often genuine efforts to make improvements. Nevertheless, the unintended effect of all the rationalization of work environments has been to squeeze out the time for creativity, judgement and thinking together about the work you are doing. Judgement is sacrificed to the fetish of routine. As Samuel Beckett wrote in his play *Waiting for Godot*: 'The air is full of our cries. (He listens.) But habit is a great deadener.'

We argue that holding time and space for controversy, exploration and renewal is not an unaffordable luxury but a critical necessity. We further suggest that for that space to be effective, it must be deliberately constructed and sustained – a significant act of leadership. Usually this means some investment, for example in setting up a new group, allowing people time off their regular work, bringing in new people or making time for open conversation and reflection. It is also essential for teams, including leadership teams, to take time out on a regular basis to stop and think about what they are doing and how they are working as a team.

At the beginning of the digital age, the boss of IBM saw the potential to develop small computers that could be used at home or the office. He also saw the difficulty of developing a business and organization focused on the new machines in a company dedicated to making and selling huge mainframe computers for large organizations. The ethos, rules and culture of the big company would kill off the new development before it even had a chance to grow. The boss's response? He set up a secret 'skunk works', entirely separate from the main business, where the normal HR and financial rules would not apply. The leader of the new unit would report to him alone. The result? The development of the IBM PC and huge success.

You need to protect innovations while they are young and fragile and ensure they are not killed off by measurement and reporting; by the rules and bureaucracy designed for well-established products and processes. Everyday managerial rules are put aside in order to allow people to step back from day-to-day pressures and focus on the strategic. People have a chance to think together, to confront difficult issues, to create and develop together and reach for what they will commit to together. You want people to experiment, to take risks, to innovate, to follow their intuition and instincts. You encourage people with different perspectives and views to speak their minds. You relish curiosity, uncertainty and 'I don't know'; you don't try to banish doubt from conversations. You judge people not on the results of experiments or pilots (you know most will fail) but on whether they were worthwhile experiments and something was learnt. New development is a process of trial and error. The ground rules are different. You have to try lots of things before you know what will work. And there is a critical role for leaders – to hold firm to the objective despite all the hubbub. What are we seeking to achieve together? What is our purpose?

Of course, while it may be necessary to separate and protect research and development from the hurly-burly of day-to-day operations, this comes at a price because it creates an 'us and them' mentality (see the IT story in Chapter 2). What the researchers discover to be effective is not necessarily welcomed or adopted by practitioners, as the world of medicine illustrates with multiple examples of best or better practice recorded in journals but not implemented.

For many of us, leading in the middle of this hurly-burly, the idea of protected time and space for discovery can seem like an unobtainable luxury. We have had to learn this in our own practice too, and as a result we often accompany leaders and groups in their workplace as they go about their normal business. This encourages leaders and groups to stop and think, if only for a few moments, about what they are doing. It means treating informal corridor conversations as just as meaningful and significant as the formal meeting with an agenda and minutes. Here are some stories of leaders who have made 'wiggle room' part of their regular work.

Connecting up the formal and informal

Andrew was a Environment Director in a borough with a million residents. Every week, he spent two days visiting various sections of the department, often getting there by public transport or on foot. He wanted to experience how well the public was served by his workforce. When he noticed a problem or some good work he talked to the relevant people. He praised those who deserved it, and sat down with those who in his eyes had been neglectful, exploring with them what they could do about their performance.

This is how Andrew made thinking spaces available at the operational level. Alongside this investment in the social capital of the department, he organized quarterly community days for the majority of the department, leaving a rotated skeleton staff to run the service on those days. On these days, different sections took turns to discuss their own work and current strategic projects on behalf of the whole department. It was up to this section, in co-ordination with the director and their own head, to organize the day. It was expected that one of the sessions would explore how well co-operation between the sections was working, and identify what people wanted more and less of from the others. Part of the day comprised a meeting of the senior management group in a 'fish bowl'. In the inner circle the director and each section head discussed 'current challenges' in their strategic projects on behalf of the whole organization, with a couple of empty chairs as part of the inner circle. Those in the outer circle, watching and listening, were free to take one of the empty chairs, offer their perspective and join the discussion.

By gathering his own experience of the service, and talking it through with staff, Andrew was connecting the formal and informal experience of organizational life. We naturally find spaces for exploratory 'meaning-making' conversations, but often they are hidden, indeed they operate underground. They happen around the coffee machine or in the pub, but not in an official setting or meeting. These exchanges are disconnected from (and often hostile to) the official discourse. The conversation will often be about the most recent example of organizational madness: 'You wouldn't believe what they are asking for now'. Such conversations help us to survive the rigours of organizational life and the tension between the formal and informal way of getting things done. The informal meetings reassure us that 'it's not just me' and represent a place of safety where we can talk about all the things that it would not be safe to talk about formally at work.

Unlike the regional government in Chapter 6 that wanted to eliminate gossip from the workplace, Andrew normalized 'gossiping' about how things were going and what needed to be addressed. By holding the occasional management group meeting in public in a fish bowl, he not only encouraged openness and transparency but normalized the management group. They were not special or different people who held themselves apart from the organization, they were in the middle of it, making sense of what was going on and what they were trying to achieve. Andrew understood that his department did not have a culture in need of rebuilding, but that he and his workforce were a living, adaptive culture.

Do you have their phone numbers?

Jennifer (Jen) is a senior civil servant. She has been working on how to improve the way policy is made in government. When she arrived in her department a number of people told her that other departments were blocking the changes that they wanted to bring about. Sometimes it was the Department of Business, sometimes it was the Treasury, sometimes Number 10, but it was always someone else. Jen talked to people about what had happened. She asked if she could go and talk to the civil servants in the departments that were 'blocking us'. 'Do you have their phone numbers?' she asked. 'No,' came the reply, 'we always deal with them by email.'

Jen got the phone numbers and talked to the people in the other departments. They said it was her department that wouldn't listen to them and had blocked things! Jen convened a meeting of the people from the different departments, not to tackle 'the problem' but to explore what different people were seeking to achieve and how they might go about it. The meeting was surprisingly positive and constructive. It was agreed that a group of civil servants from different departments should meet every month to explore how they might work together.

After several months the group began to develop suggestions on how to develop policies that were of shared interest. They began to explore how to steer their bosses and difficult personalities away from conflict and towards tackling shared issues. Over a period of nine months relationships were transformed and a more productive pattern of policy making was developed. Jen connected with others as people, not labels. She took an intelligent interest in the other person's needs and perspectives. She broke out of 'us and them' and invited others to do the same.

And now another story.

Getting over the need to be right

Karl is the boss of a regional government in a European country. He is young, ambitious and has been in post for a year. In that time he has made a few senior people redundant and encouraged others to retire. The national government has introduced new standards that need to be met. Karl says 'these are things that should have happened years ago'. There is no more money for public services, expectations are rising and the population is ageing. Things have to change.

Many of the executives in the organizations that Karl relies on to deliver services are unsettled. His predecessor had an open door and you could drop in and talk things through. There is a long history of consultative leadership in all the organizations. Things change slowly by consent, and this seems under threat.

Karl is in the middle of the world as it is, as it could be, and according to the politicians, as it should be. Like many leaders, he is at a critical point in his career. He succeeded through his intelligence, determination and ambition. He is good at sensing what needs to be done and persuading others to follow. He believes he is right. Now, as he works on a bigger stage, he is discovering that 'being right' isn't enough, and may even be counter-productive. Having the best arguments, the right data and analysis and/or a forceful personality is not enough. Others don't follow and are not sure if they can trust him. Will they be next to be sacked?

Karl is in charge but not in control. He will be held to account by the politicians and his career will be affected. He has lots of positional power and authority which has taken him so far. This positional authority has allowed him to shake up the leadership of certain departments because he had a responsibility to act. Taking action, even when it may be legitimate and necessary, has consequences too. Being right is not always sufficient.

We come across many passionate, idealistic leaders who give the impression that they enjoy battling with others. Knowing that you are right and others are wrong can be very energizing. Yet, in due course, these dynamics trap us into a world of 'us and them', or even worse, 'me and others'.

At an intuitive level, Karl is aware of this through his relationship with his political leader who is well established, powerful and sees it as his job to reform services and get things done. This leader knows he is right.

There are multiple local and national priorities, and when Karl asks which are more important he is told that they all need to be delivered. Karl knows that if he simply passes on this he will lose credibility. He knows that he has to find ways to live in the middle of this tension; to do enough to keep the politicians happy by getting 'some runs on the board' while negotiating and agreeing with his executives which of the priorities are most important, where to start and so on.

Karl needs to be able to 'stand in the shoes' of the political leaders and his executives; he needs to live with their different demands and requirements. This is not about being right, 'selling' something or demanding that 'you are either for or against us'. It is about accepting what you cannot change. Karl knows that his political leader won't change, so there is no point in an argument. Rather, he seeks to work with his executives and their organizations as a community of connected silos, as we described in Chapter 7. Karl needs the organizations to be successful in their own right, and to see themselves as interdependent, not as islands. This is a risk for Karl because he needs to trust that his executives will recognize the value of the 'wiggle room' that he is creating for them by not simply passing on the message 'do it all'. He has to trust that they will take responsibility for being part of the community. In this way, the sense of 'us and them' becomes useful and important for Karl and the executive group. They become an 'us' in part because of the over-simple, unreasonable demands that 'they' (the politicians) are imposing.

Karl had choices of course. He could have gone down the road of 'alignment', which is one of the most weasel words of organizational life, much loved by leaders, managers and consultants. Perhaps the greatest failing of the heroic orthodoxy is that it fosters compliance and not commitment. People become skilled in doing enough to tick the boxes (sometimes through manipulation and deceit), but often, while they may hit the target, they miss the point.

Playing the long game

Like many effective leaders, Karl has a pragmatic preoccupation with how to move forward while keeping in mind long-term aspirations and goals. This is the 'art of the possible' that experienced leaders know well. They are focused on getting results, here and now, and they think carefully about purpose and long-term success.

In Chapter 12 we draw together the threads from earlier chapters and summarize how to break through bonkers to recover the humanity in organizations.

CHAPTER 12

Recovering Humanity in Organizations

As we reflect on our experience of working with leaders who have made a difference, who have broken free of bonkers, we see some themes and patterns. These we summarize in this chapter.

We are sceptical of idealized, abstract templates. Context – the particular history, culture, people and circumstances that we work with – is all-important. What works in one situation does not necessarily work in another. Every situation is unique and has to be treated as such – that is the craft of leadership. What we offer here is a summary, not a recipe.

We do not claim that these themes are new; rather that they have been buried under the heroic orthodoxy landslide and we need to dig them out.

Get connected – we don't lead alone

A big theme of this book is that people do not lead alone. Instead of taking the whole burden on their own shoulders and feeling a need to do change *to* others, those who make a difference reach out and are adept at forming alliances across groups and organizations. They are more focused on developing attachments with others than getting strategies and plans right. They don't try to perfect plans in their heads but get out and negotiate with others, to develop not *my* but *our* agenda. Instead of telling others what is needed, they frame questions and name unresolved issues that invite others to join the dialogue and take responsibility. They don't battle but negotiate to find common ground and a working majority. They look for help.

Much of the time in today's organizations we are pushed towards fragmentation. Endless reorganizations, technology-based bureaucratic control and the managerial mindset, all cause disconnection between people and groups. At a time when wondrous technology is available to us that should promote connection, the social and ideological trends of the age cause us to fragment. The first job of people who want to make a difference is therefore to get connected and help others connect. This means tackling the contradiction and major cause of stress in any organization today – that outcomes depend on working together across boundaries while performance is measured individually.

Get connected

The resource we have if we want to make a difference is the relationships we have: the range and quality of our connections. People who lead effectively have strong networks; people with whom they can speak their truth and work out what is most important to them, and how to go about achieving it. In the current world of 'Permanent Transition', strong peer support and a reliable network of partners/collaborators are essential. Organizations, bosses and structures keep changing and increasingly cannot be relied upon. There is more and more to work out and make sense of; only strong relationships can meet the need.

We often see leaders trying to keep control by keeping issues to themselves or handling them one to one. Yet the solutions often lie in connecting, and tabling issues, with a group or groups. It is only the collective intelligence of the many that can tackle complex problems. It is the leader who works as a go-between, connecting top–middle–bottom and linking across specialisms and structural divisions, who is most likely to make an effective and real difference.

Individual identities are negotiated with others. People find themselves as part of something larger. We have seen people be effective because of an unusual ability to mobilize a network, to demonstrate empathy and understanding (not necessarily agreement or liking), to be themselves in an open and direct way and thereby connect well with others. Sometimes the capacity to connect well is never there or is eroded by the pressures of senior roles. Then the leadership is ineffective. Sometimes the connections are planned and the result of deliberate effort; sometimes they are unexpected and arise because of a shared interest or sense of identity that was not anticipated.

There is, of course, a limit to how many relationships we can handle. What's essential is that we work out which ones are most important, and how to develop them.

Some useful questions to ask yourself:

- How can you involve the people closest to you?

- Which individuals and communities are you reaching out to, inside and outside your organization, to discover exactly what the problem/opportunity/issue is?

- How do others see the issues? What are their needs/perspectives? How do you encourage people to express openly their feelings about the problem/opportunity/issue?

- Who is at the margin now that you should bring in to the centre of conversations?

- Who is most important to your success?

- What is the quality of your key relationships? Can you speak openly about what matters most? Can you at least exchange with others, as adult to adult? Is there mutual trust?

- How might you improve the key relationships? How can you reach out, to signal respect and curiosity? And where are your boundaries – what will you not accept?

- Are you able to say: 'Will you do this for me?'

Get real – finding our settled enough self

We cannot change the world tomorrow. What we can do is take responsibility for ourselves – and our response to others and events – today.

For all of us there is a gap between our idealized self and our true self. Getting connected enables individuals to be settled enough, aware of their limitations and able to reach out for help when it is needed. The connections enable them to be prepared but not complete; to be spontaneous in the moment and respond to people and circumstances as they arise. The connections enable leaders to regulate themselves when needed, to find out with others when they overplay a strength or don't give themselves credit for things they are doing well. What's most important now? When do they need to be kinder to themselves? When should they dig in and insist? What's less important and needs to be let go of? What do their instincts and feelings tell them? How do they check out if these impulses are correct? They can only discover these things in conversation with good, critical friends.

The prevalent heroic idealization of leaders pushes us to pretend on the outside that we can do it all, that we have the answers, while leaving us crippled and feeling imposters inside. Finding a grounded, good enough sense of self is the foundation for leading others.

We are who we are. Paradoxically, it is by facing reality as it is, not as we would like it to be, that we become more able to make a difference. There is great sense of relief to be found in recognizing and naming realities.

Get real

245

This is lifelong work. There is rarely balance or ease in people who seek to make a difference and who need to ask others to do things for them. But the engagement with themselves, their own personal history and their people, needs to be good enough. If we take on roles that don't suit us, or go against our values, we can become angry and ineffective; we can become isolated and unable to learn with and from others.

Those who lead well have enough confidence in their own judgement. Good judgement does not mean knowing, or coming up with, the answer. It is the capacity to think clearly and critically, when anxiety is high and you are in a fog; the ability to read the situation, to pick up signals, intuitively and emotionally. It means letting go of the easy certainties and engaging with the complexity of your role, making sense of what happens with those around you. It involves developing the capacity to hold together different tribes, paradigms and interests, and to gain the oxygen of different perspectives so that you are not trapped in one paradigm. It involves acknowledging that good management is essential, but effective leading comes first; the ability to work out when and how to intervene and when not to. The acknowledgement of limits, while holding on to your strongest felt ambitions; the capacity to reach a decision and act in conditions of uncertainty, knowing you will only learn by taking some (considered) risks.

Self-belief is a complex matter. We are well aware as coaches that many senior figures are driven by a need to prove themselves. We see and hear the self-doubt that many show when you get close to them. The question 'Who am I to have this leadership role?' is very common. We ask: 'What is it in yourself that you have to face?'

We would worry if there were no questioning of self and ways of working. And yet, *enough* confidence is essential, enough belief in your own capacity to influence others constructively. That confidence comes from trying things, thoughtfully, and achieving results.

Big things often take time. Endless patience and perseverance will probably be needed. What support from others will you need and how will you come to terms with your own strengths and limitations?

Now consider:

- When are you at your best? How could you do more of this?

- What are your distinctive capabilities, the shadow side of these capabilities and your limits?

- What are your demons? How are they valuable? When might you need to regulate them?

- What have you learnt from your experience?

- What do you represent for others?

- What do you hope for? What do you fear?

- What are your longer-term objectives? What's most important? What trade-offs are you willing to make?

- Realistically, what influence or control do you have? What do you have to live with?

- How do you look after yourself and keep in good enough shape to lead and influence others?

- Are you ready for the long haul? What would help sustain you?

- What should you focus on now to develop your craft as a leader?

Get going – being principled and fiercely pragmatic

Instead of pushing 'change' into the future, effective leaders take responsibility and work here and now, step by step, one meeting, one interaction at a time, to make a difference. Acting in the belief that what you do matters, that this meeting matters, that the next conversation you have might be world-changing in some way is at the heart of what it takes to make a difference. What's the small change in behaviour or action that could shift the way you work and the impact you have?

Get going

Successful leaders recognize that the world does not go according to plan, and that they can't think their way to success; they need to try all sorts of stuff and then step back to review honestly what has worked and what hasn't. They are willing to have a go at different things and see what they can learn. It is the experience of new ways of working and new results that energizes them, and others, to go further.

Successful leaders recognize the need for 'runs on the board' – results in the short term that demonstrate that progress is being made and win the confidence of sceptics. They work with the short, medium and long term in mind; and they don't confuse them. What can I nudge forward today – and what should I leave for another day? It's a matter, again, of good enough judgement. Substantial results often require time and constancy of purpose.

Those we see making a difference are principled *and* pragmatic. They have a backbone; they know what is most important to them (what they should insist on) and what is less important. They have a strong sense of purpose, of values and principles. With that, they are able to be *fiercely* pragmatic. They know where their red lines are and where they are not. They are able to be themselves and express themselves and thereby can tune in to the needs and wishes of others.

Successful leaders acknowledge that organizations are communities with histories and cultures, politics and dynamics of their own. They treat them with respect and are curious about how they work and why things happen. They do not destroy existing practices or institutions just for the sake of it. With others, they consider what works well, what does not work so well, and what needs to be improved. They pose clear questions and are cautious about simple answers. They appreciate what has gone before and the work people have done, even as they set out the case for changes. They ask: 'How do we maintain and develop what is special about this organization?' They define specific issues to work on and say why; and they recognize and accept that objectives and priorities will change as work proceeds.

They accept that there will always be some things that they do not understand and in that sense are 'sublime', to use Edmund Burke's word.

We meet many people in organizations who feel overwhelmed. The 'to do' list seems endless; there are too many emails waiting for an answer and still there are the new initiatives coming down from above that they don't know how to respond to. 'I'm full up, I have no time for this' is a cry we often hear. Sometimes people say they can't cope with the day-to-day operational challenges, much less find time and space to think about the bigger issues that their instincts tell them need to be tackled. And sometimes, faced with the managerial orthodoxy, taking the initiative can seem too much of a risk.

Interrupt the email tsunami

Thus it is vital to have space, with others, to step back and think; to avoid being consumed by the bureaucracy and box ticking; to get those above you off your back, enough; to keep some perspective and retain some 'wiggle room'; to weigh up the risks. Remaining trapped on a hamster wheel of 'chop, chop, busy, busy' activity seems less attractive when you step back and get some perspective. Above all, thinking together with critical friends provides the opportunity to 'see with new eyes', to discover that there are other ways of seeing the issues and new ways of working and achieving results.

Some questions:

- What's working well, what not so well and what needs to change?

- What's special about your organization and how can you sustain it?

- What seeds of the new are there in the present?

- How do you maintain and/or create 'wiggle room' for discovery?

- How can you rein in the excesses of the heroic orthodoxy and the managerial mindset?

- What is the current problem/opportunity/issue, exactly?

- What is the action or experiment that you should try today and in the next few days and weeks?

- What different conversation or interaction is needed now, and how can you help bring it about?

- Who should you enlist to help with the action or experiment?

- How will you know if your experiment is successful?

- What 'runs on the board' do you need to show soon?

- How could you use yourself differently, to have a different impact?

- How could you be kinder to yourself?

We cannot break free of bonkers on our own. What we do has intended and unintended consequences. Small shifts in behaviour and action can make a big difference, but we won't see the potential or understand how to realize it without connecting well with those around us. We are all caught up in the spirit of the age. We need to help each other to recover the humanity in organizations.

In Conclusion

In this book we offer the words to talk about what is bonkers in today's organizations: what is happening, the impact it has and what we can do about it.

We live in an age when 'economic man' and marketization reign supreme; when, too often, idealized models have replaced trust and judgement; when relationships and experience are deemed to be of no importance (for example in competitive tendering when selecting a supplier); when endless transitions are mistaken for transformation; and when feelings and intuition are neglected. We live in an age when what matters is not what works in practice, but what works in theory.

Any great idea (including the heroic model), taken too far, becomes damaging. We stop thinking, we stop feeling, and we stop using our antennae to judge what is needed now. We disconnect from colleagues and friends because we are no longer interested in listening seriously. We have our certainties and simple formulae and believe they must be obeyed. So it has been with the idea that people are economic animals, to be prodded and persuaded by incentives and penalties, systems and metrics, carrots and sticks. But we are not donkeys!

We live in a world of unintended consequences. The strange, unintended consequence of all the talk about transformational leadership, change and strategy has been to bury us all in more and more cack-handed bureaucracy. Good-quality bureaucracy – efficient and effective rules and processes – is essential in any organization. What we have now, however, is more and more people spending time filling in forms, going through the motions and losing sight of what their organizations are for.

In this book we have sought to recover wisdom about how to lead in organizations; wisdom that has become buried under the heroic orthodoxy. We do not seek to replace one set of easy certainties with another. We argue for reconnecting leadership, change and strategy in organizations with the rest of human culture. They are not (as some management consultants and business schools would have us believe) islands that we can find only with their expensive help. They are part of what we do as humans. We want to restore humanity to how people are at work; to push back at the dismal idea that the only guide is one version of economics devoted to free markets, choice and competition.

Break free of the economist's tunnel vision

Breaking free

It is time to break free of the heroic orthodoxy. We don't have to be victims; nor do we need to fall for the destructive fantasy that, in order to lead, we need to be charismatic individuals driving through change. If we have responsibility in organizations, we need to avoid both the cries of despair and the siren voices suggesting we should be superheroes.

If we feel oppressed and bewildered by what is going on in our organization, the first thing is to step back and stop and think, with others. We need to recover the capacity to think and feel; to gain some perspective; to see more clearly what is going on in our situation. The heroic approach has normalized the absurd. If we step back, we see how crazy it is to spend so much time constantly reorganizing, ticking boxes, meeting the requirements of badly designed computer systems and pretending to do valuable work. We need to remind ourselves of what is most important to us, to our colleagues and our organization. The sense of relief, if we can speak our truth, is enormous.

Humans are distinguished from other primates by their capacity to reflect on their experience, learn from it and decide how to adjust to changing circumstances. This capacity needs to be developed and encouraged, not closed down, as it is in too many organizations.

We need to be sceptical of grand ideas and universal prescriptions and work, step by step, to address complex challenges. We should value experience and judgement and be respectful of the wisdom accumulated in long-standing institutions. We need to reassert that there is no one answer – companies and organizations do not have a special morality and statecraft derived from the doctrine of 'economic man'. What we have to do is 'deal with the problems . . . with the application of as much intelligence as one can muster, guided by ordinary morality', as British politician William Waldegrave asserted in his 2015 memoir.

We need to seize the moment, to experiment, to try things out and reflect on the results. We need to foster the craft of leading, our intuition and understanding about what makes a good experiment, and our ability to judge the results. We need to let go of the idea that the answer is 'out there', in a business school or management guru. We need time out to stop and think with peers and critical friends. We need safe (enough) spaces in which people can say what they think and express what they feel. We should avoid the idealistic abstractions that have become such a trap. We should be as specific and direct as we can in saying what works, what doesn't work, and what needs to be improved.

We should get serious about our humanity at work. We need to value and respect organizations as communities. The foundation for learning well from experience is the social fabric of institutions – the connections between people, the quality of relationships, the trust and respect between individuals and groups, the sense of shared objectives and values. This needs at least as much attention as the formal roles and responsibilities, the metrics, visions and strategies that the orthodoxy focuses upon. The social fabric needs to be respected, valued and upheld, as circumstances change. The social fabric existed before us, and provided we do not inadvertently destroy it, it will outlive us. It may often be intangible but it is nonetheless important for that.

In support of learning from experience, we need a realistic, down-to-earth sense of what 'good enough leading' is. The job of leading is not (usually) to come up with the answer yourself – it is to be curious, to embody values and aspirations, to set an example for others of what is needed. It is about getting the right people in the room (not too many, not too few, to get a range of perspectives), asking good questions, and helping others have the necessary conversations. It is about trusting your people – enough of them have the skills, experience and qualities to take initiative and responsibility if you let them, so free them up!

Leaders need to be (much of the time) in the middle, not at the top, connecting up organizations and people, and helping them find meaning in their work.

We need to trust ourselves. We need to work with others to find our settled (enough) selves and discover who we are as part of something larger. We should be aware of the emotions that drive us and not seek to hide from (or deny) them. Emotions are the source of commitment and innovation.

We should stop pretending that everything depends on the leader. We need to recognize that a leader can do little on their own. We need to see how much a leader can do if they acknowledge seriously their interdependence with others.

What stops us?

What stops us naming the bonkers and getting back to the real work? Often it is fear. We fear the consequences for our jobs, income or position if we push back against the orthodoxy.

It is difficult to take responsibility ourselves (and to encourage others to take responsibility) when we are faced by so much uncertainty and complexity, made worse in organizations by the permanent upheavals. People feel insecure and disturbed. It is natural to want to keep your head down and hope it all will pass. However, the result would be more organizations failing to learn and adapt; eventually they would die.

A sense of shame also stops us challenging the absurd. The heroic orthodoxy is pervasive – it gets inside us; and it leads to a sort of false self. We find ourselves acting and speaking in ways that are strange. This can produce powerful feelings of guilt and shame.

We work with leaders who seem split – they are talented and engaging people, yet under pressure they shut down and revert to the orthodoxy.

We can break free

What is an example of someone leading in the way we suggest? Angela Merkel, chancellor of Germany, is often called 'Europe's most influential leader', yet is not obviously charismatic. She can seem like a technocrat but she also connects as 'Mutti' (Mum) with many voters. Her leading is rooted in her life history growing up as a pastor's daughter in communist East Germany. She knows that all ideologies can become a trap, and she experienced the extraordinary moment when ordinary people came together in 1989 and made the peaceful revolution that ended communist dictatorship in her own country. Merkel is famously pragmatic and slow to reach conclusions. She settles herself by consultation and gathering the evidence. As a scientist (she was a quantum physicist before entering politics) she knows when to abandon a hypothesis that is not supported by the data and go back to the beginning. And she knows when to dig in and insist. When challenged in 2015 about letting refugees into Germany, she said: 'I lived a long time behind a fence; it is not something I wish to do again.'

We live in a period of turbulence – socially, economically and politically. Post-Brexit and post-Trump, many people feel disturbed. Old certainties are being challenged. The consensus and capitalism that has held the peace in the West is faltering.

We are not soothsayers, we do not know what will emerge, but what we can see is that the heroic orthodoxy is under great strain. Cracks are showing.

Andreas Whittam Smith, founder of the *Independent* newspaper in the UK, speculates that 'after a 40-year period when it was thought that governments knew best (roughly late 1930s to late 1970s), followed by the belief that markets knew best (late 1970s to roughly now), I hope we shall come to a new dispensation: people know best.'

What impresses us is the number of people who are going on working and leading productively, despite the bonkers consequences of the heroic orthodoxy. Every day we see people doing good work, despite the orthodoxy. We want to celebrate and honour those people and encourage them – you – to do more by taking responsibility and acting with integrity, in the thick of complexity and uncertainty.

More than 200 hundred years ago, Edmund Burke, the politician and philosopher, said that the social order:

'is the result of the thoughts of many minds in many ages. It is no simple, no superficial thing, nor to be estimated by superficial understandings. An ignorant man, who is not fool enough to meddle with his clock, is, however, sufficiently confident to think he can safely take to pieces and put together, at his pleasure, a moral machine of another guise, importance and complexity, composed of far other wheels and springs, imbalances and counteracting and cooperating powers. Men little think however immorally they act in rashly meddling with what they do not understand. The delusive good intention is no sort of excuse for their presumption.'

More than 60 years ago, the British politician Aneurin Bevan talked about the need 'to eschew absolute prescriptions and final decisions'. He was concerned that, faced with complex issues, people become either missionaries for simple solutions or 'vacillate, that is give up, do nothing'. His remedy? 'Passion in action in pursuit of qualified judgements' – in other words, avoiding simple solutions but coming to a judgement about what a complex situation requires and being prepared to act vigorously to support your judgement.

Bevan's words seem more relevant than ever today. Progress towards specific goals is often complex and messy. It may not be easy to see what is needed. Different, and sometimes contradictory, ideas and interests have to be held in mind at the same time. The unexpected has to be expected. Constancy of purpose and patience and determination can produce what is needed. We have the opportunity in the conversations and interactions we have in today's organizations to connect with others and make a difference. We can break free of bonkers!

Appendix

A Short History of the Heroic Orthodoxy

'Practical men, who believe themselves to be quite exempt from any intellectual influences, are usually the slaves of some defunct economist.'

John Maynard Keynes, *The General Theory of Employment, Interest and Money*

So where has this orthodoxy come from?

It is a set of ideas, beliefs and assumptions that business schools and consultancies around the world (but particularly in the United States) have offered in the last 40 years. The key words are leadership, change and strategy. The ideas offered under these headings link together to form a powerful paradigm.

The ideas were a reaction against the stagnation and conflicts of the 1960s and 70s. It was argued that the public sector had become too large, and that companies, trade unions and bureaucracies defended their own interests at great cost to the health and wealth of society as whole. The later collapse of communism, and the extraordinary rise of China and other new economies having embraced market economics and globalization, seemed to show that the ideas were part of the march of history.

Heroic leadership

As organization consultants, we are struck by how often we meet the heroic ideas of leadership – an idea of how leaders ought to be.

The key elements of this picture of leadership are heavily influenced by the American, individualist tradition – one great person (usually a man) heroically wrestling a company or organization into shape. As we described in our previous book, *Living Leadership*, this view says that, to be a leader, you need to be:

• Visionary.

• Inspiring – an outstanding communicator.

• Able to make things happen – leading with 'steely resolve'.

Warren Bennis . . . The shadow of the great man

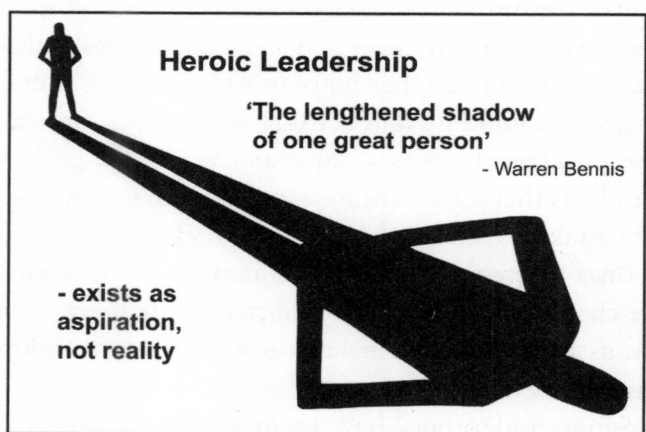

Since we wrote the first edition of *Living Leadership* over 10 years ago, this model of heroic leadership has not changed much, and remains dominant. Our research shows that it is now tempered by more concern about how leaders work with employees to generate shared commitment to change – there is a lot of attention paid to 'Engagement Management'. However, the essentials have not changed.

The picture of leadership is an instrumental one – leaders *doing things to* their company or organization. The leader stands outside their organization; they know the way forward and they struggle heroically to make the organization understand and implement the path they have identified. Their job, over a period, is to drive through fundamental change.

The spotlight is on the heroic individual – their qualities, experience and understanding; their determination to drive through change. The clear message is that the strength and capacity of the leader are the decisive factors.

In recent years, a number of leadership authorities have challenged the heroic orthodoxy. Professor Ronald Heifetz at Harvard has offered some valuable insight into other ways of seeing leadership. He says that 'in a crisis we tend to look for the wrong sort of leadership. We call for someone with answers, decision, strength and a map of the future; someone who knows where we ought to be going – in short, someone who can make a hard problem simple.' But the critical problems are often not simple. 'Instead of looking for saviours we should be calling for leadership that will challenge us to face problems for which there are no simple, painless solutions; problems that require us to learn new ways of acting.'

Heifetz makes a critical distinction between technical challenges – ones where there are known answers – and what he calls 'adaptive challenges', where we have to learn new ways of acting and new assumptions and behaviours in order to address the problems.

Peter Senge and others have argued for the importance of collective leadership. In his article 'The dawn of system leadership', Senge calls for leaders who have the capacity 'to see the larger system' and develop 'a shared understanding of complex problems'. They need to foster 'deep, shared reflection' and 'generative conversations' that allow groups and individuals to hear others' points of view. He suggests that trust must be built in order to foster 'collective creativity'. He draws on the organizational learning literature to highlight the need to 'face difficult truths about the present reality' and learn how to use 'the tension between vision and reality to inspire truly new approaches'.

At the same time, in our work as organization consultants, we notice that the heroic orthodoxy is alive and well in the minds of many people in authority. Whatever some academics may argue, the notion of the heroic leader – 'that's how *I ought to lead*' – remains stubbornly resilient.

Heroic change

There are a myriad change frameworks and tools from different consultancies and business schools to choose from, but what they have in common are these ideas:

- Change is the only constant. We live in a time of unprecedented change and the pace of change is speeding up. Adapting to change in your environment becomes ever more important.

- Change won't happen unless you push, and push hard. Organizational change is difficult. Cultures won't move unless they are forced to – they have enormous inertia. Also at the individual level, people don't want to change. They will want to keep things as they are. They will defend vested interests.

- The job of leaders is therefore (and this has superseded all other ideas of leadership) to 'drive' change. The change meant is not just a shift in a payroll system or new ways of purchasing stationery, it is changes in culture – the distinctive patterns of thinking and behaving in different organizations.

- Organizational change is complex and difficult to realize. Meticulous preparation and discipline and effective planning and programming are required to ensure that change is 'delivered'.

- All the different aspects of organizations (as described, for example, in the often used McKinsey '7S' model) need to be 'aligned'. If any one element is out of alignment with the others, your change process will not be successful.

A notable example – and the most often cited – of the management and leadership tools supplied by the business schools in support of the dominant paradigm is that provided by John Kotter, the now retired Harvard professor.

Kotter advocates an eight-step process for leading change. It starts with creating a sense of urgency – the famous 'burning platform'. He talks about 'crafting and using a significant opportunity as a means for exciting people to sign up to change their organization'. The clear assumptions are that change is good and that people won't want to change unless you 'excite them'.

The next step in Kotter's process is to 'build a guiding coalition'; to 'assemble a group with the power and energy to lead and support a collaborative change effort'. Note the insertion in recent years of the word 'collaborative', a recognition that change needs to be led by many people, and that relying on one figure at the top won't work.

Next comes the 'vision' word, so beloved of managers and consultants. The job is to 'shape a vision to help steer the change effort and develop strategic initiatives to achieve that vision'. The vision must be communicated with passion, and repeated endlessly.

There follows what sounds like simple common sense – remove obstacles, create quick wins and build on your momentum.

But there is a fly in the ointment. According to Kotter, 70 per cent of change programmes don't work. Other gurus and consultants suggest the number may be 80 per cent or higher – unless, of course, you use their (perhaps expensive) expertise!

There is a surprising dearth of evidence about the impact of change programmes, but what is often asserted is that most don't work.

Kurt Lewin's change management model

Kotter's process and much of the literature on 'change management' have their origin in the work of the German émigré Kurt Lewin. Just after the Second World War, Lewin proposed three stages to change:

Unfreeze – getting ourselves and others ready to change; discovering the motivation and using techniques such as Force Field Analysis to articulate the pressures for and against change.

Change – the transition period; the process or 'journey' we undertake towards the new way of being. It can be scary, and we need support, Lewin argued.

Refreeze – ensuring the change is reinforced and sustained into the future and finding a new stability.

In today's world of constant upheaval, many people have doubted that the third (refreeze) stage ever arrives. However, the idea of the three stages and the different psychology required has been very influential. Much modern practice focuses on what is needed at different points to get groups to 'buy in' to change.

'Resistance to change'

A vast literature has grown up about 'resistance to change', and how to 'overcome' this resistance.

The 'formula for change' is one interesting example of this literature. Developed by Richard Beckhard and David Gleicher, and refined by Kathie Dannemiller, it provides a formula for assessing whether a particular change programme is likely to succeed. It states that for organizational change to be effective:

$$D \times V \times F > R$$

D = Dissatisfaction with how things are now

V = Vision of what is possible

F = First, concrete steps towards the vision

R = Resistance

In recent years the advocacy about top-down change has been moderated by humanistic concerns (see for example the 'Transition Curve') and the perceived need for 'Engagement Management'. However, the belief in the need 'to drive change from above' remains intact.

Programming the future

Also in recent years, a new band of consultants has emerged. Typically, strategy consultants will produce a great strategy but leave you unsatisfied when it comes to implementation. This new group of consultants seek to fill the gap. They will programme manage the implementation and change that you need. They will 'drive through transformation'. They will connect with key managers and help them think through the skills and resources needed, and they will identify the activities and steps necessary to 'execute the strategy' – the critical business of translating strategic aspirations into doable plans. They will 'galvanize teams'. They will monitor and control 'delivery'. They will convert the uncertainty associated with strategy into tightly organized programme management. In this way, you can seek to programme and control every aspect of the future of your company or organization, and wish away the uncertainty and contention that, as we describe in Chapter 4, comes with strategy.

Heroic strategy

The passion about the need to lead change is supported by the orthodox view of business strategy. Again, there are many varieties to choose from (as set out in Henry Mintzberg *et al.*, *Strategy Safari*).

There are important differences between different groups of management gurus and consultants. Some, like the grandaddy of modern business strategy, Michael Porter at Harvard, give priority to getting your thinking straight; being absolutely clear about what the objectives of your organization are and the basis on which you compete with other companies or organizations. Once you are clear about what your competitive advantage is, you need to 'align' (that word again!) your organization ruthlessly around that advantage. If lower cost is your advantage (as, say, in Ryanair), every aspect of your organization needs to reflect that priority. If, on the other hand, superior value to customers (as say for BMW) is your competitive edge, every part of your organization needs to support that priority. Many years of sustained application and discipline are needed for companies or organizations to be champions in their chosen discipline.

Michael Porter had the brilliant idea of inverting the logic of modern economists. While economists explored how to develop free markets, as a better (and morally superior) way of allocating resources, Porter argued that the job of business is to subvert markets and make money by putting obstacles in their way. Truly free markets would lead to lower profits for everyone. To make money, therefore, in a sustained way, you must do what you can to limit competition. Careful thinking and analysis are needed, Porter says, if firms are to see how best to subvert the market.

Key words and phrases for this group are 'analysis', 'quality of thinking', 'alignment' and 'discipline in implementation'.

Another group of business strategy 'gurus' emphasize the need for imagination and re-inventing companies and organizations.

For Gary Hamel or the 'Blue Ocean' proponents, W. Chan Kim and Renée Mauborgne, analysis of the status quo is not of much use. What is needed is radical thinking that reimagines and reinvents what a company or organization does. This approach is about seeing the 'big picture' in quite a different way from others. The task is not to battle existing competitors but to make bold moves, to seize 'white spaces' or 'blue oceans' of uncontested market space. Classic examples are Google, Facebook or Spotify. Many of these companies are of course internet developments. There is frequent mention of 'first-mover advantage' – once you have seized the uncontested space, it may be very difficult for anyone else to challenge what becomes a dominant position or de facto monopoly.

The differences in approach are important; lively debates continue between the different strategy schools.

Yet the similarities are also striking. They have contributed key elements to the dominant orthodoxy:

- A few people (usually at the top of organizations and often with the help of outside consultants) develop the strategy – the thinking about how a company or organization should succeed. Only they have the necessary intellect, breadth of vision, concern for the interests of the organization as a whole and willingness to grasp the nettle.

- Clarity of thinking is essential. Strategy is about choice of direction and priorities. If the thinking is woolly or blinkered, the strategy will not be good enough.

- The strategy needs to be written down so that it is clear and can be communicated to all parts of the company or organization, and everyone knows their part in it. The strategy also needs to be communicated to stakeholders such as investors so they understand where the leadership of the organization is heading.

- Effective implementation (or 'execution' as it is called, without any sense of irony) is key. Many strategies, it is said, fail because they are never properly implemented. The job of middle managers and front-line staff is to 'deliver' on the agreed strategy. Strong 'performance management' and careful planning and programming are needed to ensure effective implementation.

Shareholder value – one value above all others

Another key element that the business schools and consultancies have contributed over the last 35 years is development of shareholder value as the dominant, espoused goal of business.

This school asserts that the aim of management can be expressed in the single metric of increasing shareholder value. As Matthew Stewart says in his book *The Management Myth*: 'The idea is that all leaders have to do is to ensure that management does what it is supposed to do . . . by aligning it with the market, by rewarding it for maximizing shareholder value.'

In one bound, all the complexities of conflicting interests and objectives are wished away. Management theory and free market ideology are fused together; it is a potent and far-reaching combination.

The triumph of free market ideas

There is one remaining piece of the jigsaw. The heroic orthodoxy is linked to the triumph in the political world over the last 35 years of neo-liberal ideology – the idea that the free market is not just a better way of running economies but a morally superior way to organize society. If you allow people freedom, they will have to make choices and take responsibility themselves. The choices that institutions and countries make will be better as a result.

It is free market ideas that provide the impetus for many would-be transformational leaders to drive through social change from above.

It is assumed that change toward the free market is required. 'Reform' has come to mean movement towards the market. Parties of the political Right have been colonized by free market ideology and those of the Centre and Left have failed to come up with a coherent alternative.

There is an interesting contradiction in the application of neo-liberal ideas. What if not enough people want the greater economic freedom advocated by the free marketers? What do you do then? Do you have to force people to be 'free'? As David Marquand points out in his book *Mammon's Kingdom*, one of the contradictions of the Thatcher years in the UK was the extent to which central government took control and weakened other institutions in order to 'set the people free'. In the same way, Andrew Lansley's 'reforms' of the NHS had to be pushed through by diktat from above.

Notes on Sources

Most of this book is based on our experience and research as organization consultants and executive coaches. We also draw on the following books, articles and websites (directly and indirectly) and suggest them for further reading.

Chapter 1

Binney, G., Williams, C. Wilke, G. (2012 third edition) *Living Leadership: A practical guide for ordinary heroes*, Pearson Education
Goffee, R. & Jones, G. (2006) *Why Should Anyone be Led by You? What it takes to be an authentic leader*, Harvard Business School Press
Graeber, D. (2016) *The Utopia of Rules*, Melville House
Mintzberg, H. (1989) *Mintzberg on Management*, Free Press
Oshry, B. (2007 second edition) *Seeing Systems*, Berrett-Koehler
Vollmer, L. (2016) *Zurück an die Arbeit*, Linde Verlag

Chapter 2

Goffee, R. & Jones, G. (2006) *Why Should Anyone be Led by You? What it takes to be an authentic leader*, Harvard Business School Press
McGilchrist, I. (2009) *The Master and his Emissary: The divided brain and the making of the western world*, Yale University Press
Meyerson, D. & Scully, M. (1995) Tempered radicalism and the politics of ambivalence and change, *Organization Science*, Vol. 6, No. 5
Norman, J. (2014) *Edmund Burke: The visionary who invented modern politics*, William Collins

Chapter 3

Brooks, J. (2001 new edition) *Thank You Comrade Stalin!: Soviet public culture from revolution to cold war*, Princeton University Press

Norman, J. (2014) *Edmund Burke: The visionary who invented modern politics*, William Collins

Waugh, E. (2000) *Brideshead Revisited*, Penguin Classics

Wordsworth, W. (1888) 'The Prelude', from *The Complete Poetical Works*, Macmillan

Chapter 4

Bungay, S. (2010) *The Art of Action*, Nicholas Brealey

Department of Health (2006) Best Research for Best Health: A new national health research strategy, Department of Health

Goold, M. (1992) Design, learning and planning: a further observation on the design school debate, *Strategic Management Journal*, Vol. 13

Mintzberg, H. *et al.* (1998) *Strategy Safari*, Prentice Hall

Mintzberg, H. (1994) *The Rise and Fall of Strategic Planning*, Prentice Hall International

Moltke, H., Graf von, *Militarische Werke*. Vol. 2, Part 2, found in Hughes, D.J. (ed.) (1993) *Moltke on the Art of War: Selected writings*, Presidio Press

Pascale, R.T. (1984) Perspectives on strategy: the real story behind Honda's success, *California Management Review*, Spring

Pascale, R.T. & Athos, A.G. (1986) *The Art of Japanese Management*, Simon & Schuster

Tolstoy, L. (translated by R. Edmonds) (1982) *War and Peace*, Penguin Classics

Winterson, J. (2012) *Why Be Happy When You Could Be Normal?*, Vintage

Winterson. J. (1985) *Oranges Are Not the Only Fruit*, Pandora

Chapter 5

Tillich, P. (2014 third revised edition) *The Courage to Be (The Terry Lectures)*, Yale University Press

Chapter 6

Binney, G., Williams, C. & Wilke, G. (2012 third edition) *Living Leadership: A practical guide for ordinary heroes*, Pearson Education
Fox, K. (2005) *Watching the English: The hidden rules of English behaviour*, Hodder & Stoughton
Handy, C. (2002 new edition) *The Age of Unreason: New thinking for a new world*, Random House Business
Owen, H. (2008) *Open Space Technology*, Berrett-Koehler

Chapter 7

Burke, E. (edited by L.G. Mitchell) (2009 reissue edition) *Reflections on the Revolution in France*, Oxford University Press (Oxford World's Classics)
Block, P. (2009) *Community: The structure of belonging*, Berrett-Koehler
Caldarelli, G. & Catanzaro, M. (2012) *Networks: A very short introduction*, Oxford University Press
McGilchrist, I. (2009) *The Master and his Emissary: The divided brain and the making of the western world*, Yale University Press
Norman, J. (2014) *Edmund Burke: The visionary who invented modern politics*, William Collins
Senge, P., Hamilton, H. & Kania, J. (2015) The dawn of system leadership, *Stanford Social Innovation Review*, Winte
Timmins, N. (2015) The Practice of System Leadership, The King's Fund
Uhlig, P. & Raboin, W.E. (2015) *Field Guide to Collaborative Care*, Oak Prairie Health Press

Chapter 8

Arendt, H. (1976) *The Origins of Totalitarianism*, Harcourt Brace Jovanovich
Binney, G., Williams, C. & Wilke, G. (2012 third edition) *Living Leadership: A practical guide for ordinary heroes*, Pearson Education
Burke, E. (1770) Thoughts on the Cause of the Present Discontents, printed for J. Dodsley
Dahrendorf, R. (1979) *Society and Democracy in Germany*, W.W. Norton
Drinker Bowen, C. (1986) *Miracle at Philadelphia*, Back Bay Books
Kahane, A. (2010) *Power and Love: A theory and practice of social change*, Berrett-Koehler

Reitz, M. & Higgins, J. www.hbr.org/2017/04/5-questions-to-ask-before-you-call-out-someone-powerful

Tillich, P. (1954) *Love, Power and Justice: Ontological analyses and ethical applications,* Oxford University Press

Chapter 10

Block, P. (2009) *Community: The structure of belonging,* Berrett-Koehler

Chapter 11

Beckett, S. (2006) *Waiting for Godot: A tragicomedy in two acts,* Faber & Faber

Brueggemann, W., quoted by Rebecca Solnit in the *Guardian,* 16 July 2016

Heifetz, R. (1994) *Leadership Without Easy Answers,* Harvard University Press

Mead, M. (1963) *Sex and Temperament in Three Primitive Societies,* HarperCollins

Popova, M. www.brainpickings.org

Solnit, R. (2016 updated edition) *Hope in the Dark: Untold histories, wild possibilities,* Canongate

Timmins, N. (2015) The Practice of System Leadership, The King's Fund

In Conclusion

Bevan, A. (1977) *In Place of Fear,* EP Publishing, found in Marquand, D. (2015) *Mammon's Kingdom,* Penguin Books

Norman, J. (2014) *Edmund Burke: The visionary who invented modern politics,* William Collins

Qvortrup, M. (2016*) Angela Merkel: Europe's most influential leader,* Gerald Duckworth & Co.

Waldegrave, W. (2015) *A Memoir. A different kind of weather,* Constable

Whittam Smith, A., After Brexit, we do need a new political party – just not like the ones we've already got, *Independent,* 4 April 2017

Notes on Sources

Appendix

Beckhard, R. (1987) *Organizational Transitions*, Addison-Wesley

Bennis, W. & Nanus, B. (1985) *Leaders: The strategies for taking charge*, Harper & Row

Binney, G., Williams, C. & Wilke, G. (2012 third edition) *Living Leadership: A practical guide for ordinary heroes*, Pearson Education

Drucker, P. (1978) *Adventures of a Bystander*, Harper & Row

Gawande, A. (2015) *Being Mortal*, Wellcome Collection/Profile Books

Hamel, G. & Prahalad, C.K. (1994) *Competing for the Future*, Harvard Business School Press

Heifetz, R. (1994) *Leadership Without Easy Answers*, Harvard University Press

Keynes, J.M. (1936) *The General Theory of Employment, Interest and Money*, Palgrave Macmillan

Kim, W.C. & Mauborgne, R. (2005) *Blue Ocean Strategy*, Harvard Business School Press

Kotter, J.P. (1996) *Leading Change*, Harvard Business School Press

Lewin, K. (edited by Martin Gold) (1999) *The Complete Social Scientist*, American Psychological Association

Marquand, D. (2015) *Mammon's Kingdom*, Penguin Books

Mintzberg, H. *et al.* (1998) *Strategy Safari* Prentice Hall

Norman, J. (2014) *Edmund Burke: The visionary who invented modern politics*, William Collins

Peters, T. & Waterman, R. (1982) *In Search of Excellence*, Harper & Row

Porter, M.E. (1985) *Competitive Advantage*, Free Press

Senge, P., Hamilton, H. & Kania, J. (2015) The dawn of system leadership, *Stanford Social Innovation Review*, Winter

Stewart, M. (2009) *The Management Myth*, W.W. Norton

Acknowledgements

It is said that it takes a village to raise a child, and the same could be said for this book. In our 'village' are clients, colleagues and our families. All the client stories in this book are anonymized, apart from those relating to the National Institute for Health Research (NIHR). We are particularly grateful to the NIHR (Professor Dame Sally Davies, Dr Russell Hamilton and Dr Louise Wood) for their permission to tell their story from our perspective. We are also grateful to our many anonymized clients from whom we have learnt so much. We hope to have done justice to your leadership.

For several years we have been part of a consulting team and without them this book would not have happened. We particularly thank Sarah Beart, Janet Smallwood, Isabelle Read, David Birch, Hugh Pidgeon, Michaela Rebbeck, Tsheli Lujabe and James van Oosterom (whom we miss very much). Your challenge, encouragement, ideas and empathy have sustained us. Thanks too to John Higgins for getting us going. James Baylay drew the pictures that accompany the text. His flexibility, enthusiasm and insight are much appreciated.

Finally, thanks to our families for their encouragement and forbearance, particularly when we have been, literally and metaphorically, miles away in the book.

Thanks to the whole 'village'. We accept that any mistakes are ours alone.

About the Authors

George Binney

I read history at Cambridge, trained as a barrister and have an MBA with distinction from INSEAD. Important for me is the critical thinking I absorbed while studying history. I am passionate about bringing a historical perspective to issues. What's the context for this issue? How has it come about? Another influence is working as a manager and director in two big companies – GEC and Courtaulds – as well as at McKinsey. I have a profound respect for good management, for people who get things done in complex and turbulent worlds. A third influence is my experience as an organization consultant. I specialized first in strategy, then in organizational change and now in leadership. I am fascinated by the interplay of practice and theory and how to make sense of what leaders and managers actually do.

Philip Glanfield

I studied theology at Leeds which taught me about doubt and thinking critically about how we live our lives. I qualified as a social worker and worked as a probation officer for a number of years before, via an MBA, moving into the NHS. There I was a director in a hospital and worked regionally and nationally. In my last NHS post I led a team working with struggling organizations. My Ashridge Masters in Organization Consulting grounded my intuition and experience in theory and provided the final encouragement to go into independent consulting. In this work I am drawn to organizations that seek to add social as well as economic value. I enjoy working with individuals, teams and organizations which are prepared to start from the premise that what they do, individually and collectively, matters and can change the world – while accepting that, because the world is complex and beyond our understanding, what they, and I, do may not make a difference.

Gerhard Wilke

Having managed and salvaged the family business in my very early years, in my early 20s I decided to get educated and came to the UK. As a mature student I studied Social Studies at Ruskin College, Oxford and then Social Anthropology and Social Science at King's College, Cambridge. Subsequently, I worked as a lecturer in London, specializing in work with mature students from ethnic minorities. In mid-career I became a group analyst and built up my own consultancy. As a post-war German, I am sceptical about heroic and visionary leaders. As an anthropologist I learnt to consider what is taboo in an organization. I learnt how communities can find the glue which holds them together, and why they should do so. With some confidence I can claim that I have helped individuals and groups in many organizational contexts – from engineering, property, banking and law to state institutions – make explicit what is implicit, make what is stuck come unstuck, and find a very different way of looking back and ahead.